"Here's a straight-from-the-shoulder guidebook that avoids the shallows of world-think, anchors to the rock of God's grace-filled and loving ways, and answers the deep-seated heartcry of innumerable honest men and women, teens and collegians who are seeking lasting fulfillment."

JACK W. HAYFORD
president, the King's University

"Joy is hugely important in the lives of believers, and this is the perfect manual for finding real happiness."

ANDY ANDREWS
New York Times bestselling author of *The Traveler's Gift* and *The Noticer*

"Randy Robison challenges us to think more deeply about what it means not only to be joyful but also to be happy. The result is a book that will awaken the desire for true happiness in your life—today and always!"

MARGARET FEINBERG
author of *Scouting the Divine*

"This book makes war on the age-old heresy that Christians are unhappy people. Redeeming the truth that our God is the author of joy, Robison breathes life again into his reader's soul."

JOHNNIE MOORE
author of *Honestly*
vice president and campus pastor, Liberty University

"We thoroughly enjoyed reading this book. It is very well written, practical, thought provoking, and relevant. A great resource for a godly view of true happiness."

Major League All-Star JOSH HAMILTON and his wife, KATIE

"Having dedicated my life to strengthening marriages, I understand the importance of happiness for couples. This book not only helps people individually but also creates a better foundation for all relationships. In *God Wants You to Be Happy*, Robison joins godly wisdom with personal insight to create a refreshing guide for living with unconditional joy and happiness."

JIMMY EVANS
CEO, MarriageToday

"Is there an unhappy person in your life? This book will help point the way to a place of greater joy."

DR. KEVIN LEMAN
author of *Have a New Kid by Friday* and *Have a New You by Friday*

"Negativity and discontent just don't lead us to the lives we desire. Wouldn't we rather just be happy? I would, and I know you would too! Robison shows us we all can possess and express happiness. What an impact this could have on every family, marriage, and individual."

JENNIFER ROTHSCHILD
author of *Self Talk, Soul Talk* and *Lessons I Learned in the Dark*
founder, Womensministry.net and Fresh Grounded Faith Events

"This book has the potential to change a lot of lives! Real happiness can only be found in the light of Christ. This light, implanted into the heart of every believer, longs to consume us and emanate from us. Robison clearly defines the differences between the alluring happiness based on chasing our self-centered, ego-driven, materialistic desires, and happiness based on the light of Christ already within us."

PETE WILSON
author of *Plan B*

"Robison provides an in-depth look at what happiness means in God's economy— he really has given us a Bible study on the subject. God does want us to be happy in the truest sense of the word. I learned so much and appreciate Randy's new insights, his scholastic approach, and his practical applications. If you want to know happiness as God intends it, read this book!"

RUTH GRAHAM

"This is a marvelous message for the perilous times in which we live. It is a must read for anyone in pursuit of true happiness."

KELLY WRIGHT
TV news anchor/reporter

"In troubled times, Robison reminds us that "the joy of the Lord" isn't just part of a verse to quote—it's God's central plan for our lives. The choice is ours to walk in happiness, and Randy illuminates the steps!"

CAROLYN CASTLEBERRY
author of *It's About Time* and *Invest Yourself Where It Matters*

"True happiness isn't achieved through selfishness. Rather, it comes from seeking God first and living a life that blesses others. Robison gets that. I'm so thankful for a book that reveals how to live with a biblical happiness that not only enriches your own life but also impacts the lives of those around you."

ROBERT MORRIS
senior pastor, Gateway Church
Southlake, Texas

GOD
WANTS
You to Be
HAPPY

JAMES RANDALL
ROBISON

HARVEST HOUSE PUBLISHERS

EUGENE, OREGON

GOD WANTS YOU TO BE HAPPY
Copyright © 2012 by James Randall Robison
Published by Harvest House Publishers
Eugene, Oregon 97402
www.harvesthousepublishers.com

Library of Congress Cataloging-in-Publication Data
   Robison, James Randall.
   God wants you to be happy / James Randall Robison.
     p. cm.
   ISBN 978-0-7369-4946-0 (pbk.)
   ISBN 978-0-7369-4948-4 (eBook)
   1. Happiness—Religious aspects—Christianity. I. Title.
   BV4647.J68R63 2012
   241'.4—dc23

                       2011025154

Printed in the United States of America

12 13 14 15 16 17 18 / BP-NI / 10 9 8 7 6 5 4 3 2

I am blessed by many who choose to give me great joy, starting with my wife, Debbie, and children, Abbie, Alek, Aidan, and Audrey. This includes my parents and my sisters' families, the Redmons and Turners, and my friends at the Met Church and the men of ORU's Youngblood.

CONTENTS

INTRODUCTION

God wants you to be happy. It's a simple idea, but a complicated reality. About a year after the horrible genocide in Rwanda, I traveled to that hellhole to document the construction of a new orphanage for the television program *LIFE Today*. I found children who had been maimed, traumatized, and separated from their families. But I also found something unexpected: children who seemed to be genuinely happy. No doubt they had shed many tears and had a few more coming, but most of them were not gloomy, angry, or detached. They played, sang, and enjoyed the company of their fellow orphans.

I also met Fred Nkunda, a Ugandan man who exuded joy despite the conditions of poverty, political strife, overwhelming need, and long hours of working for a pittance to care for his children. A few years later, he succumbed to cancer, but while he lived he wore a warm smile as he selflessly gave himself to others. The same was true for a young Canadian couple and the African Christians who devoted their lives to the mission work.

When I came home, I noticed a shocking contrast. Most Americans lacked the joy that those Rwandan children and mission workers undeniably possessed. Despite the affluence, modern conveniences, political stability, and endless other material blessings, people here scowled, exhibited impatience, and simmered with discontent. How could this be?

Somewhere along the way, many of us in America have lost something. We have failed to experience happiness—real happiness that comes from within and flows to others. And it's not just missing in "the world." It's in short supply in our homes, businesses, and churches.

Too often, happiness is viewed as a circumstantial condition. It is actually a personal character trait. We understand the necessity of love, peace, patience, kindness, goodness, faithfulness, gentleness, and self-control. These are accepted and desirable consequences of Holy Spirit residency. But happiness? It is easily overlooked or dismissed as unattainable in this life.

From a biblical perspective, happiness holds the same status as these other virtues. It is not the goal of a relationship with Christ, but it is a promised by-product. Of course, we need to establish the meaning of happiness to believe such a claim, but when we examine the scriptural notions of happiness, joy, delight, and other related concepts, a part of God's plan for His children becomes clear: He wants us to be happy.

If you consider yourself a happy person, as I consider myself to be, then you will find this book to be enlightening and encouraging. You will understand yourself better and learn how to get really good at being happy. And I will warn you now: Happiness is infectious. The better you are at it, the happier people around you will be, which will make you even happier.

If you doubt your happiness or readily admit that you are unhappy, the ideas and scriptures laid out in this book will open the door for you to escape your darkness and enter the light. The journey may be difficult, painful, and exhausting, but it will be worth it—not just for you, but for everyone in your life. You have no idea how much your life can change and how much you can change the lives of your loved ones when you become a truly happy person.

James tells us that if we are suffering hardships, we should pray, and if we are happy, we should sing praises (James 5:13). If you are suffering, pray as you read through this book. God wants to bring you to a place where you are so happy, you can't stop yourself from singing. It may sound ridiculous now, but that's the incredible difference God wants to make in your life!

Most of us, happy or not, have an awareness gap. We spend time pursuing things we think will make us happy, but we don't consciously consider the true meaning of happiness. If we examine the idea (both analytically and scripturally), discover its true meaning, recognize the obstacles, and actively pursue the paths to happiness, it can become a distinguishing characteristic of our lives—as it should be.

I became aware of this gap in my life many years ago. It took a long time for me to habitually consider how my words and actions impact my happiness and that of those around me, but I think I have made some progress. In this journey, I have discovered an incredible secret every believer should know: Happiness is a choice. It is a gift from Jesus Christ that we can own and then learn to give away. In His word, God repeatedly tells us to rejoice—an action that can create happiness. So be prepared to discover true happiness, learn how to keep it, and begin to share it with others.

God wants you to be happy. And in His word, He shows us how.

Our Calling to Be Happy

*God cannot give us a happiness and peace apart from
Himself, because it is not there. There is no such thing.*

C.S. Lewis, *Mere Christianity*

Why should you be happy? Few people would actually admit that they prefer being unhappy. Yet many people do things that invite unhappiness. It can be a nasty, self-perpetuating habit. I suspect most people don't engage in much self-examination or put too much thought into the subject. Subconsciously, everyone wishes for happiness, but few make it a daily practice to ask, "Will this make me more happy or less?"

My church asked me to coordinate a band for a summer youth Bible study. The pastor in charge gave me a general idea of what they wanted and encouraged me to do what I wanted to do. So I did. I hustled up a great group of singers and instrumentalists. After the first weekend, the sound technician told me that what we had done did not fit his "vision." I asked the lead pastor whose vision was operative—mine or the sound guy's. He replied that mine was, with the guidelines he and I had already agreed on. So I planned for the next week.

On the Thursday before the second Sunday session, the sound technician told me I couldn't use all of the singers. Again, I went to the lead pastor. It took a day, but the lead pastor came back and, apologetically, asked me to scale down. I was in the uncomfortable position of having to kick someone off the stage—someone who had volunteered and prepared for the weekend. Obviously, I was not pleased.

I had a choice to make. On one hand, I could complain, point at others' deficiencies and lack of communication, and generally cause a ruckus. In my mind, I was justified. I even had other band members on my side. But what good would that do? As I squelched my emotions and conformed my mind to God's word (and this book, which I was writing at the time), I realized that my reaction would impact a lot of people. I could easily hurt the tech guy. I could divide the band members from the youth leadership. I might even make a few people look bad. What good would that do?

Stirring discontent would not make my volunteers happy. It wouldn't make the youth workers happy. It wouldn't make the pastor happy. And it sure wouldn't do anything positive for the kids who showed up and needed to be ushered into God's presence through the praise music. In the long run, it would work against my happiness too. I spent many years building the self-confidence, the musical ability, the relationships with other musicians, and the trust of church staff to lead worship. Torching others would set me back regardless of how "right" I thought I was.

So I stabbed my pride in the back, buried my ambitions, and bit my tongue. I focused on the positive things and thanked everyone involved for their role. I trusted God to move in the students' lives regardless of how the music sounded. As a result, everyone was happier—including me.

As Christians, we are called to be happy and infect others with happiness. Let's consider three compelling reasons to seek godly happiness.

You Are the Light of the World

Our happiness affects everyone around us. Perhaps you have a parent, spouse, or child who is perennially unhappy. How does that affect you? Does that person make you want to sing praises? I doubt it.

"You are the light of the world," Jesus said. If you are a believer, He was talking about you. Discontent, bitterness, depression, and every other enemy of happiness does not brighten a room, much less the world. In fact, it has the reverse effect.

We all know people who elevate the mood when they walk into a room, and we all know people who bring it down. Happiness in you will create an environment for happiness in other people. It's not guaranteed—those people have their own free will—but light dissipates darkness. If we are to be the light of the world, as Jesus declared, we need to start by being the light at home, at work, or wherever we are. Happiness is a light. It brightens everyone's day.

Salvation and Joy

Even more important, we have something that overrides every obstacle to happiness: salvation. That made all the difference for the prophet Isaiah. "I delight greatly in the LORD; my soul rejoices in my God. For he has clothed me with garments of salvation and arrayed me in a robe of his righteousness" (Isaiah 61:10 NIV). Other versions replace *delight* with *rejoice, find joy in,* or *will be full of joy.*

The Hebrew word is *sows* or *suws*, depending on your resource. The same word is used in Psalm 119:162: "I *rejoice* at Your word, as one who finds great spoil." In God's word, we find the way to eternal salvation. Through salvation, death and sin are defeated. *Spoil* does not refer to bad mayonnaise. It refers to the treasures recovered from a defeated army. One of the spoils of this spiritual war (which is already won) is victory over sorrow, suffering, bitterness, fear, and every unhappy emotion. Because of the cross, happiness can extend beyond any passing pain of this life.

"Weeping may stay for the night, but rejoicing comes in the morning" (Psalm 30:5 NIV). The pain of this world is temporary, but the happiness of God's salvation through Jesus Christ lasts forever. The work of salvation does not begin when we die. It begins when we are born again. So if you have been born again, you are entitled to the spoils of war, including happiness. You can find joy in your salvation now.

Our Witness in the World

If you are a Christian but constantly convey unhappiness, you are undermining your effectiveness as a witness for Christ. Who wants to be like an unhappy person? Consider the case of the Westboro Baptist

Church in Wichita, Kansas. This group is famous for picketing the funerals of American soldiers. Brandishing signs such as "Thank God for Dead Soldiers" and "God Hates Fags," this small band of malcontents has inflicted misery on grieving parents, cost cities thousands of dollars in security, and embarrassed the entire Christian community. These people do not produce the fruit of the Holy Spirit any more than a walnut tree produces watermelons. They repel believers and nonbelievers alike. Who wants to be like them!

In the same way (though less blatantly), when happiness is not a characteristic of your life, other people are not attracted to whatever you have. If you are an unhappy believer, people quickly draw this logical conclusion: "He or she is a Christian and is miserable. Why would I want to be like that?"

I like Merriam-Webster's definition of *fruit* in the context of the fruit of the Spirit: "a condition or occurrence traceable to a cause." The Holy Spirit in our lives is the cause; joy is the condition. One is directly traceable to the other. We are called to bear the fruit of the Spirit, so we are called to possess happiness. Whether you are happy for your own sake, for the sake of your loved ones, or for the sake of your Savior, you have reason enough to put thought and effort into being happy.

To ignore this is to miss the mark God has for your life. Whether by omission or by the tolerance of things that crush happiness, to live an unhappy life is, to a great degree, to fall short of Jesus' plan for your life.

HAPPINESS IS...

*My advice is...try to recapture happiness in
yourself and in God. Think of all the beauty that's
still left in and around you and be happy!*

ANNE FRANK, *THE DIARY OF ANNE FRANK*

The entire premise of this study depends on an accurate definition of happiness. Unfortunately, the word has suffered a tragedy of the English language, as has the word *love*. I love my wife. I love chocolate chip cookies with almonds. And we wonder why people ask, "What is love?"

A brief survey will provide you with a litany of poetic, sublime, and sophomoric definitions of happiness. Here are a few:

- "Happiness is two kinds of ice cream" (*You're a Good Man, Charlie Brown*).

- "Happiness ain't a thing in itself—it's only a contrast with something that ain't pleasant" (Mark Twain).

- "Happiness Is a Warm Gun" (the Beatles).

- "Happiness Is...Quilting!" (tagline at happinessisquilting.com).

So what is happiness? At www.GodWantsYouToBeHappy.com, you'll find an in-depth survey of the language and relevant scriptures, but the short version is this: The answer depends on what you're talking about.

Let's start with the English word *happy*. It comes from the Old Norse word *happ*, meaning "good luck." One of Merriam-Webster's definitions derives from the original: "favored by luck or fortune." We would say, "I happened to be the one-millionth customer, so I won a free gift." It means lucky. There is a scriptural parallel in the Hebrew, but we translate it as *blessed*. Of course, the biblical context implies a source of the good fortune rather than mere chance. Those of us who believe that "the steps of a man are established by the LORD" (Psalm 37:23) tend to view good things in life as blessings from God, not just random luck. That is not the primary focus of this study, though God's blessings certainly justify our happiness.

The irrelevant definitions include such idioms and expressions as *impulsive* (a trigger-happy cop), *irresponsible* (a punch-happy boxer), *obsessed* (a stats-happy announcer), and *notably fitting* (a happy choice for dinner). None of these have scriptural relevance to true happiness.

Instead, the closest English definition of biblical happiness would be "characterized by well-being and contentment." Yet even that is insufficient. My teenage sons are content to play video games all day long, but a life of that would not make them happy. To the contrary, it would most likely make them fat, unhealthy, antisocial, poor, and miserable. The most appropriate definition I can offer comes from *Barnes' Notes on the New Testament*: happiness is "a state of mind free from trouble." That comes from the Greek word *euthymō*, which means "to be joyful, be of good cheer, of good courage."

Think about that idea. Has your mind ever been free from trouble? Wouldn't you be truly happy if your mind was untroubled by anything? I tend to think so. That isn't to say ignorance is bliss. Rather, we can fully know what is going on around us and yet trust God and His promises enough to not be troubled by those things.

As much as I like that definition, it is still lacking. Some things *should* trouble us to varying degrees. We should have a burden for those who do not know Christ. We should be bothered by the plight of the poor, downtrodden, and sick. We should "weep with those who weep" (Romans 12:15). Things that are not right in the world or in our lives should trouble us so we are motivated to corrective action. And therein lies some of the irony.

Our burden for the lost should cause us to preach the gospel, which brings great joy. Our concern for the poor should prompt us to care for them, which brings great joy. Our dissatisfaction with sickness causes us to seek cures, which brings great joy. And so goes this dynamic of seemingly opposing forces that is crucial to our happiness. As we find our place in God's plan and obey His will in our lives, we often address disturbing problems and find happiness in offering the solution.

Billy Graham obviously exhibited a great burden for the lost. But instead of being despondent over those he didn't reach, he found great joy in preaching salvation. Missionaries I have met in places like Rwanda and China clearly live in constant discontent with the condition of those to whom they minister. Simultaneously, they are happiest when working in the capacity in which they are called. Ask full-time missionaries what makes them most unhappy, and many will point to the time they must spend on furlough taking care of domestic issues or raising more money to fund their work. They would rather be in the field with those who suffer.

One final connotation that helps to shape a proper definition of happiness comes from the Hebrew word *'ashar*. It means "to advance, to make progress." Attaining and maintaining happiness is not a one-time, all-inclusive effort. It is a series of choices that move us in the right direction.

Words may be insufficient to fully express the concept of happiness or joy, but you generally know whether or not you have it. The purpose of this book is to make you more aware of happiness and its impact on you and those around you, to minimize the obstacles, to define the biblical paths to happiness, and to help put "mixed blessings" in perspective. One day, nothing will stand in the way of complete joy for those who are in Christ. And even now, in the midst of our struggles, we can (and should) experience genuine joy. Our lives will be touched by trouble, but our minds can still remain free.

Happiness and Joy

Early in my life, I was taught in church that happiness and joy were two different things. Happiness, the story goes, is purely emotional. It depends on external circumstances. It comes and goes with the fortunes of life. Joy, on the other hand, is internal. It's more spiritual. It supposedly sticks with you even when you're completely unhappy.

This makes no sense unless your definition of happiness follows the Old Norse meaning of luck. I don't relate to this kind of happiness, and I don't know anyone who does. Common sense should tell us we can't be joyful and unhappy at the same time. If that's the case, then our emotions are ruling us, not our minds or spirits—and certainly not God's word.

If I ask whether you are a happy person, you don't reflect on your immediate circumstances and ignore the totality of your life. If you're honest, you go to your core state of mind. You may have won the lottery yesterday, but even that doesn't guarantee your happiness today. (I've seen an interesting documentary on this subject. An amazing number of people who have come into large sums of cash actually multiplied their misery.) Your true state of happiness reflects your overall joy in life.

Another definition of *rejoice* is "to give joy to." When we pair joy with "a state of happiness," we see that we can give happiness to others. Scripture backs this up. I believe this is paramount to understanding happiness: We should embrace it, possess it, and give it away.

Consider the actions to which we are called as Christians. When we share the gospel, we introduce people to a happier life. When we feed the hungry, we create happiness. When we care for those who suffer, we bring some happiness into painful situations. When we love one another as Jesus commanded, others are usually happier, and we are too. When you read the word *rejoice* in scripture, you can often insert the words *create happiness*.

Jesus said, "Therefore you too have grief now; but I will see you again, and your heart will rejoice [*chairō*], and no one will take your joy away from you" (John 16:22). The prophet Zephaniah said to God's people, "Shout for joy [*ranan*], O daughter of Zion! Shout [*ruwa'*] in triumph, O Israel! Rejoice [*samach*] and exult [*'alaz*] with all your heart, O daughter of Jerusalem!" (Zephaniah 3:14).

Jesus came to make His joy full in us here and now (John 15:11; 16:24; 17:13). Insisting that Christians can possess that joy while radiating unhappiness is either a trick of the language or a devilish lie. I believe it's the latter. It's like saying we can have the rest of the fruit of the Spirit but never actually show it. You cannot exhibit hate and say you have love. You cannot commit cruel acts and claim kindness. And you cannot be an unhappy person and pretend you have joy. Joyful people will be happy people.

Original Languages

The Old Testament includes more than two dozen Hebrew words that directly relate to being happy, glad, joyful, or delighted. The New Testament incorporates about half a dozen Greek roots. The words and connotations vary somewhat, but they are consistently expressed as a state of mind designed to be characteristic of God's people.

Perhaps the most revealing aspect of the Greek and Hebrew study is the fact that happiness is most often expressed as a noun or verb, not an adjective. In other words, it is something we do or possess, not something we feel. If we define happiness as our level of pleasure regarding something, we are hopeless. If our emotions determine our happiness, we will be maddeningly unstable. But if happiness is something we express through our actions, words, thoughts, and intentions, no external situation has power over it. Once we control it, it is an actual thing with substance and weight that cannot be taken from us unless we give it up. We possess it and express it, and no other force on earth can contest it.

Unfortunately, modern translations make it difficult to quickly assess the biblical meaning of happiness. I started with the New Living Translation, but after running into numerous passages where the word *happy* did not transliterate into the original language (it was not actually there, it was merely inferred), I opted for the New American Standard Bible and New International Version. Our English isn't like the English spoken in 1611, so I don't have much use for the King James Version, although it tends to stick closely to the manuscripts available at the time without too much embellishment. The point is, a scriptural representation of happiness cannot be obtained from a few cursory passages or single translation.

For example, if I tried to use Ecclesiastes 5:10 in the NLT to refute the idea that money can buy happiness, I would quote, "How meaningless to think that wealth brings true happiness!" The NIV says, "Whoever loves wealth is never satisfied with their income." I will make that argument in a later chapter, but it would be somewhat dishonest to not point out that a word for *happiness* does not actually appear in the Hebrew.

Similarly, the NLT renders Luke 6:24, "What sorrow awaits you who are rich, for you have your only happiness now." The Greek word translated as *happiness* is *paraklēsis*, which is rarely rendered as *happiness* in most translations. The NASB says, "Woe to you who are rich, for you are receiving your comfort in full." So even though the word *happiness* appears in the NLT, it's simply not there in the Greek. Such English variations would confuse a study of specific words without comparing the original texts.

So throughout this book you will see the original Hebrew and Greek words noted in the scripture references. A fuller survey of these words is available at www.GodWantsYouToBeHappy.com. The purpose is to convey a better understanding of the biblical concept of happiness and the direct correlation between passages that employ the same word in the original languages.

This is a big topic. It is prominent in scripture and important to God. It affects us spiritually, emotionally, and physically. We tend to approach happiness from a purely emotional perspective, but understanding it spiritually and mastering it intellectually will transform your mind and greatly improve your life.

PART 1

OBSTACLES TO HAPPINESS

Many emotions and attitudes decrease our happiness. They war against all that is good. As sure as a virus must be destroyed for the body to be healthy, these things must be purged from our hearts and minds if our joy is to be made full.

Human Nature

Strange indeed is human nature.

Sir Arthur Conan Doyle, *The Valley of Fear*

Cartoonist Walt Kelly wrote, "We have met the enemy, and he is us." He had it partially right. His application of the idea was wrong, but our human nature can be our own worst enemy and our biggest inhibitor to happiness. We are all born into sin, so we are corrupt from birth. Thus the need to be born again.

In the early twentieth century, American theologian Cyrus Scofield popularized a theological position called the trichotomy of man. It is somewhat debatable, but it has helped me understand our ongoing struggle against our own sinful nature even after experiencing salvation. Here is a simplistic explanation of the position:

Just as God is a three-part being (Father, Son, and Holy Spirit), man is made up of three parts (body, mind, and spirit). Some use the term *soul* in place of the mind, but both terms generally include one's thoughts, will, and emotions.

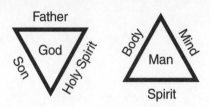

Another way of viewing the trichotomy of man is with three concentric circles. Martin Luther drew a comparison between this idea and the Old Testament temple, connecting the outer court to the flesh, the holy place to the mind/soul, and the holy of holies to the spirit.

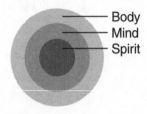

In his popular study Bible, Scofield wrote, "Because man is 'spirit' he is capable of God-consciousness, and of communication with God (Job 32:8; Psalm 18:28; Proverbs 20:27); because he is 'soul' he has self-consciousness (Psalm 13:2; 42:5,6,11); because he is 'body' he has, through his senses, world-consciousness."*

Additional parallels are drawn to suggest that Jesus Christ redeems our spirits at the point of salvation, a singular event that becomes a part of our past. The Holy Spirit works sanctification in our mind/soul in the present, and the Father will receive our bodies in glorification in the future.

I don't wish to defend a particular theological position, but I do find the concept useful to understand the daily battle that Christians fight. Clearly, our spirits need to be saved. The part of us that is dead in sin must be made alive in Christ. This is salvation and, once experienced, resides in our core being.

The part that relates to our happiness is the sanctification process. The apostle Paul referred to this when he wrote, "Work out your salvation"

---

* The Scofield Study Bible (New York: Oxford University Press, 1909), p. 1270.

(Philippians 2:12). This process stems from our spirit—the joy of salvation. The more we align our minds with our spirits, the happier we are. The more we align our thoughts, will, and emotions with our flesh, the less joy we experience.

Paul also addressed this struggle by saying, "For the good that I want, I do not do, but I practice the very evil that I do not want" (Romans 7:19). The good that he wanted to do flowed from the redeemed spirit within. The evil that he practiced was prompted by the flesh—something we all have until we physically die. The battleground, then, is in the mind.

I believe this is what Jesus referenced when He admonished His disciples in Gethsemane, "Keep watching and praying that you may not enter into temptation; the spirit is willing, but the flesh is weak" (Matthew 26:41).

When we are redeemed in Christ, the Holy Spirit dwells within us. Yet our flesh also lives, and it presses against this reborn spirit. We must renew our minds daily in order to align our thoughts, will, and emotions with the Holy Spirit. We experience happiness as "a mind free from trouble" when our minds are aligned with our spirits, not our flesh.

All of us know from personal experience that even after we are saved, we are still capable of horrendous sin. This is why Paul admonished us to avoid allowing grace to become an excuse to sin. "For you were called to freedom, brethren; only do not turn your freedom into an opportunity for the flesh" (Galatians 5:13).

Living according to the flesh is especially miserable for believers because it produces an inner conflict that nonbelievers do not experience. The unredeemed spirit lives in harmony with the flesh, but the saved spirit wars with the flesh. If the spirit is dead in sin, a deceived, deviant, and distorted mind is not only logical, it's unavoidable. Christians must take up the cross daily and die to self. We must kill our old nature.

Helen Keller wrote that "true happiness is not attained through self-gratification, but through fidelity to a worthy purpose." Of course, a blind and deaf woman knows nothing of the self-gratification that comes through two of the most predominant senses. But she was right nonetheless. And we are happiest when that "worthy purpose" is the kingdom of God.

Once we recognize that our sinful nature is a barrier to happiness, we understand that death to self is not really painful sacrifice, but liberation from a life of misery. It is not loss, it is gain. Finding the happiness at the other end of that process opens our eyes to the truth that Jesus proclaimed. Fighting what the apostle Paul called the "good fight of faith" (1 Timothy 6:12) allows our spirits to thrive, tempering the destruction of the flesh and unleashing the blessed fruit of the Spirit, including joy. Exhibiting all of the fruit, including peace, patience, kindness, gentleness, love, and faithfulness, conveys happiness to others in our lives, perpetuating the circle of joy.

Deceit

You don't have to teach children to lie; they will do it on their own. Lying is natural. And it's an enemy of joy. "Who is the man who desires life and loves length of days that he may see good [*towb*]? Keep your tongue from evil and your lips from speaking deceit" (Psalm 34:12-13).

Honesty comes only through a born-again spirit and continuously renewed mind. The Scottish poet Sir Walter Scott wrote, "Oh what a tangled web we weave, when first we practice to deceive!"

Deceit is joy's snare, causing all manner of grief. Believers who engage in deceit, including self-deception, give in to the worst of fleshly desires. A deadly array of corruption blossoms when we concede to this temptation. We must consciously avoid the mirage of comfort in lies and build on a solid foundation of truth.

DISOBEDIENCE

Now-a-days children no longer obey, they do
according to their own fancy, because they
consider themselves cleverer than their parents.

BROTHERS GRIMM, *HOUSEHOLD TALES*

I don't like rules. In fact, I hate being told what to do. Yet I was never an overtly disobedient child. I have no great testimony of falling away and then returning like a prodigal son. Instead, I learned how to not get caught. In some ways, this can be more difficult to correct than open rebellion.

So for the longest time, I could not relate to passages like this one: "Make me walk in the path of Your commandments, for I delight [*cha-phets*] in it" (Psalm 119:35). I dismissed this as nice poetry. If I had written this psalm in my teens, it would have said, "I'll try to live by your suggestions if I feel like it." By early adulthood it may have read, "Help me keep some of your rules because I know it's the right thing to do." But *delight* in it? I found it much more preferable to live by my own rules.

The word *chaphets* is a verb. It's an action. It means "to take pleasure in." The precondition is to walk (to move steadily forward) in the path (a course taking us from one place to another) of God's commandments (a code of wisdom). The psalmist is telling us to keep moving forward on the path of God's code of wisdom and we will find pleasure. That makes much more sense than trying to stick to a set of enigmatic rules.

Later in the same psalm, the writer says, "Trouble and anguish have come upon me, yet Your commandments are my delight [*sha'shua'*]" (Psalm 119:143). *Sha'shua'* is a noun: "the object of enjoyment." During difficult times, God's ways bring us a happiness that has substance. We can hold it and keep it, even while experiencing "trouble and anguish."

The problem with this is that we are all wired to do our own thing. Upon entering this world, we have our own codes of conduct. They vary from person to person, but we all have one thing in common: Our ways are not God's ways. Living by God's commandments is not natural. His ways are higher, so we need a supernatural enabling to rise above our sinful nature.

Paul wrote, "For I know that nothing good dwells in me, that is, in my flesh; for the willing is present in me, but the doing of the good is not. For the good that I want, I do not do, but I practice the very evil that I do not want" (Romans 7:18-19). Unfortunately, I have always been able to relate to this passage! I truly want to love my wife, but I don't always act like it. When I don't, I am not happy. I want to be involved in my children's lives, but I have repeatedly blown opportunities to spend time with them. When I realize it, my joy decreases.

From the time Paul was born again, he at least had the knowledge of this struggle. "The willing" existed in him through salvation. But sin still fought against "the doing of the good." This is the core of disobedience: knowing what is right and not doing it. Paul continued, "For I joyfully [*synēdomai*] concur with the law of God in the inner man, but I see a different law in the members of my body, waging war against the law of my mind and making me a prisoner of the law of sin which is in my members" (verses 22-23).

I am largely aware when I am not walking the path of God's wisdom. When I am not doing what I know I should, I am not happy. I no longer find joy in doing what I know I should not do. Like Paul, I still struggle with obedience, but I do not war against God's will. I search for it and long for it. Now I understand the psalmist when he said, "I delight [*chaphets*] to do Your will, O my God; Your Law is within my heart" (Psalm 40:8).

Go East, Young Man

One of the classic tales of disobedience in the Bible is the story of Jonah. It's the brief account of a man who heard from God and literally ran the opposite way. God told him to go east across the land, so he went west across the sea. A terrible storm hit the ship, and the other passengers believed they were being chastised by a god. Needless to say, they were not very happy about it. Jonah's disobedience had a negative effect on those around him, as disobedience often does. When they confronted him, he told them that he served the God of the Hebrews, which terrified them even more. They knew God's reputation. Then Jonah made a wonderful confession. He said, "I know that this terrible storm is all my fault" (Jonah 1:12 NLT)

Jonah didn't lie about it or make excuses. He didn't blame God. He didn't see a therapist who put the responsibility on his parents. He didn't even fault his ex-wife (if he had one). He admitted his own disobedience. Later in the story he continues to be cantankerous and argumentative, but at least he is honest. That's a great place to start for each of us.

Paul's idea of a new self speaks to the core of disobedience. "Consider the members of your earthly body as dead to immorality, impurity, passion, evil desire, and greed, which amounts to idolatry. For it is because of these things that the wrath of God will come upon the sons of disobedience" (Colossians 3:5-6). Disobedience begs the wrath of God, which is obviously not a pleasant thing.

We experience delight in obedience, but we experience judgment as a result of disobedience. In Jonah terms, happiness lies to the east and misery to the west. Walking in disobedience will never lead to anything good. That's why we must turn around and go the other way, which is the classic definition of repentance.

If you are unhappy, measure that against your obedience. Are you Jonah, running from God's path and caught in a storm? There is no joy or peace in disobedience—only trouble and discontent. God's commandments are not a set of arbitrary rules designed to keep you under His great cosmic thumb. They are the path to happiness, a way of wisdom that brings liberty. Living by your own rules is not independence; it is imprisonment. Remove disobedience from your life, and you will remove a major obstacle to happiness.

Wickedness

Of the ungodly person, the Bible says, "The words of his mouth are wickedness and deceit; he has ceased to be wise and to do good [*yatab*]" (Psalm 36:3). The Hebrew word translated *wickedness* is sometimes translated *trouble* or *sorrow*. The verb *to do good* also means "to be glad or joyful." A lifestyle of disobedience is wickedness, sorrow, and folly. It prevents goodness, gladness, and joy.

Those who give in to daily disobedience cannot find true happiness. It is one thing to strive against our sinful nature, to "fight the good fight of faith." But acquiescence to sin and ungodliness defines a wicked lifestyle. In this, there will never be any joy.

3

Bitterness

An angry skipper makes an unhappy crew.

Rudyard Kipling, *Captains Courageous*

You cannot be happy and bitter at the same time. Bitterness poisons everything in those who hold it. It troubles the mind relentlessly. As a result, joy withers and dies.

I attended school for a short time with a guy who faced terrible tragedy in his late teens. He had grown up in a Pentecostal church that taught that one's physical health was a measure of spiritual faith. When his mother, with whom he was very close, was diagnosed with a terminal illness, the family and the church fervently prayed for healing. His mother believed that she would be healed right up to her last breath.

Her death devastated him. Others made excuses to protect their theology, but he felt betrayed by God. The doubt he expressed created a rift between him and his father, and he was eventually thrown out of the house and branded an apostate. He carried the label well, castigating all Christians and mocking God. He became one of the most miserable, bitter, and unhappy people I have ever known.

Other people carry lesser degrees of bitterness, but it is still poisonous. Divorce, job loss, health crises, financial difficulty, mistreatment, and a dozen other difficult situations can plant that seed. Once the weed starts growing, it wants to take over, choking out all that is beautiful and beneficial. The writer of Hebrews warned against its dangers: "Pursue peace with all men, and the sanctification without which no one will see the Lord. See to it that no one comes short of the grace of God; that no root of bitterness springing up causes trouble, and by it many be defiled" (Hebrews 12:14-15).

I don't believe it was an accident that this writer described bitterness as having a root. It always has a source, a cause or starting point. Anger may flash in an instant, but bitterness takes time to grow. It gets stronger the longer it grows, and it's harder to remove the deeper it goes. It defiles not only the person incubating it but also everyone around it. Like the garden untended, it spreads its ugliness, blossoming into resentment, rage, wickedness, murder, and other deadly blooms. Given enough time, nothing else will be able to grow around it. Certainly not happiness.

If you are a parent with a plot of bitterness, consider the harm you do to your spouse and children. You're choking them. Your poison is polluting the soil. Your unhappiness may already be their unhappiness. Uproot your bitterness and plant a new garden. By the grace of God, you can.

A Botany Lesson

How do you know if you have a root of bitterness? The Bible gives us a few clues. The first comes from 1 Chronicles 15—the story of David moving the ark of the covenant to Jerusalem. God's presence was returning to the people, and they prepared to worship and celebrate. Verse 29 says this: "It happened when the ark of the covenant of the LORD came to the city of David, that Michal the daughter of Saul looked out of the window and saw King David leaping and celebrating [*sachaq*]; and she despised him in her heart."

We don't know Michal's full story, but we do know three things: First, she and David once loved each other; second, she came to despise him; and third, they were never close again. Note that Michal's spite came when David was worshipping God and leading others into His presence. Had she been able to worship God too, she could not have despised him for his worship. An inability to worship is a key indicator of bitterness.

Complaining

During Job's adversity, he said, "I loathe my own life; I will give full vent to my complaint; I will speak in the bitterness of my soul" (Job 10:1). Out of his bitterness, he bemoaned his temporary state and lost all sight of eternal gratefulness for the works of God. This is what happens when we allow bitterness to consume our hearts. It illustrates Jesus' explanation of where a person's words come from: "His mouth speaks from that which fills his heart" (Luke 6:45).

The Israelites were characterized by bitterness and complaining, among other things. They complained while in captivity. Once freed, they complained about Moses' leadership. They complained right through the fulfillment of the old covenant, and their bitterness blinded them to the coming of the Messiah. Paul warned believers not to be like them, saying, "[Do not] grumble, as some of them did, and were destroyed by the destroyer" (1 Corinthians 10:10). Satan is the destroyer, and one of his weapons is the bitterness we express with our own mouths. "Be hospitable to one another without complaint," Peter wrote (1 Peter 4:9).

The cure for complaining is to shift our focus from ourselves to others (hospitality) and to God, and then to confess the truth. When we truly understand God's eternal plan and our place as His servants, we will find no cause for complaint.

When I graduated from college, I went to work for a company that specialized in direct marketing. Basically, we sent tons of junk mail. One of our clients, a televangelist, used disgraceful spiritual gimmicks to solicit donations. His tactics disgusted and angered me—and he wasn't even our worst client.

Another "minister" promised all manner of healing, wealth, and other blessings for those who sent him money. One mail piece included a prayer cloth and instructed people to hold it up to a light while they asked God how much money to send. Then they were told to go into a dark prayer closet, and God would reveal the donation amount to them, along with the eyes of Jesus. On the cloths, a pair of eyes was printed in glow-in-the-dark ink, along with a dollar amount. The amount was based on the donor's giving history. If someone gave an average of $50, the cloth was printed with a little more, such as $60 or $75.

I was complaining about this to my wife when she said something profound. "Why don't you do something about it?" She'd had enough of my griping. Talking about it was insufficient. Thank God for wise counsel!

Over the next few months, I tactfully challenged the owner of the company about these gimmicks. When it became clear that things were not going to change, I found another job. This is the positive alternative to complaining. Instead of becoming bitter over the manipulative mail, I dissociated myself from the company—and I was far better for it.

(I should point out that many wonderful people worked at that company. Through my departure, I maintained a positive relationship with them. Even when circumstances are unfavorable, we need not unnecessarily burn bridges with everyone involved. I still consider the owner of the company a friend.)

When we find ourselves in a pattern of complaining, we must ask two questions. First, is this complaint legitimate? If not, we should stop. If it is, we must ask the next question: What should I do about it? The answer is never to give in to bitterness. God truly wants good things for our lives, so we must be bold enough to follow Him and leave our complaints behind.

Antisocial Behavior

When Christians avoid other Christians or "forsake…assembling together" (Hebrews 10:25), they have usually been hurt by other people who call themselves believers. Too many times, I have heard people say, "I'm taking a break from church." This always comes from people who have been mistreated or whose expectations were unfulfilled.

My pastor says, "If you haven't been hurt by people at church, you haven't been attending long enough." His point is merely this: People are people, even at church. They are flawed and will eventually do something you don't like. The problem is that when we are hurt by people at church and react by rejecting the body of believers, we are rejecting God because of man's shortcomings. Admittedly, some churches should be avoided, but not *the* church. God's stated plan to reveal Himself to the world is through His bride, the body of believers that make up the true church. We may not always gather in buildings with a cross on the marquee, but we must not forsake other believers.

When our expectations fall hollow, we have two questions to consider. First is whether our local church actually represents a body of believers.

Some so-called churches are more like rotary clubs or social cliques. We should have enough discernment to know the difference. The second consideration is whether we are a part of a church in order to get something or to give something. If we are to have servants' hearts, we do well to express that through the church.

I have been a part of the worship team at my church for several years. During that time, several people have come and gone who expressed a discontent with their role as singers or musicians. Each time this happens, I can't help but wonder whether they are there to lead others into worship or to advance their personal careers. I realize being a team player can be tough on the ego. Most musicians like the spotlight. But if we are living in obedience and seeking to serve more than anything else, we will not be discontented however small our roles may seem.

If you are burned-out on other Christians, check your heart for bitterness. You'll probably find a seed that needs to be confessed and removed. Forgiveness may be in order. Dealing with it will not be easy, but once you do, you will find that fellowshipping with other Christians is much easier and more pleasant.

Perverse Joy

We know we are nursing bitterness when we take pleasure in other people's hardships. "Do not rejoice [*samach*] when your enemy falls, and do not let your heart be glad [*giyl*] when he stumbles," we are instructed (Proverbs 24:17). This is not a statement against justice, but a warning against finding a perverse joy in the downfall of men, all of whom God loves and Christ died to save. The next verse says, "Or the LORD will see it and be displeased, and turn His anger away from him." It breaks God's heart when people fail. Rejoicing in their failure puts us on the wrong side of God's will, which is that they should repent and be restored to Him.

Nowhere is this practice more celebrated than in politics. When Ted Haggard was the pastor of a large church and head of the National Association of Evangelicals, he helped rally support for a Colorado amendment preserving marriage between one man and one women. When his homosexual activities came to light, there was unabashed celebration among many gay activists. A similar glee was seen on network news following the revelation that the daughter of Sarah Palin, a vocal advocate of family values, turned up pregnant out of wedlock. Happiness in the downfall of others is not true joy; it is bitterness expressed through mockery. This false joy is clearly different from genuine happiness.

Gossip

Happy people don't like to bad-mouth others, but bitter people find great satisfaction in criticizing others behind their backs.

After the flood, Noah took up farming. He planted a vineyard but enjoyed the wine a little too much. Genesis tells us that he "uncovered himself inside his tent" (Genesis 9:21). He was drunk and naked—perfect fodder for gossip. His youngest son, Ham, saw his father and promptly spread the word. But Shem and Japheth, Noah's two other sons, took a garment and walked backward into the tent to cover their father. "Their faces were turned away, so that they did not see their father's nakedness" (verse 23).

This is the difference between a godly reaction and gossip. David wrote about this type of behavior by noting how his enemies "aimed bitter speech as their arrow, to shoot from concealment at the blameless" (Psalm 64:3). Gossip is a form of bitter speech.

Nobody is perfect. We all make mistakes and will witness the mistakes of others. The question is whether we will "uncover" people by talking about them or help them in their "nakedness" by covering their shame. "Above all, keep fervent in your love for one another," the apostle Peter wrote, "because love covers a multitude of sins" (1 Peter 4:8). Love does not excuse, justify, or ignore sin. But it doesn't gossip about it.

A prime example of this occurred when a person I know was caught in a particularly disturbing sexual sin. The easy tendency was to talk about it. Of course, there was a level of communication necessary in dealing with the fallout, but I was impressed to note the reaction of those closest to him. Nobody hid his sin—to do so would have been complicity in the crime—but even while he was in prison, his friends never stopped showing him the love of God. The last I heard, he was repentant, honest, and seeking personal restoration. Justice was not thwarted, but neither was love.

When we are filled with love, we will cover the mistakes of others, even when they are exposed. Gossip finds no place in this scenario. But when a root of bitterness springs up, the desire to bring others down by spreading their shame flourishes. If gossip flows freely from your mouth, check your heart for bitterness.

Lack of Grace

The cardinal scripture on bitterness also mentions one other attribute: grace. "See to it that no one comes short of the grace of God; that no root of bitterness springing up causes trouble, and by it many be defiled" (Hebrews 12:15).

Bitterness and grace are like oil and water; they don't mix. Interestingly, the Greek word for *grace* is *charis*. It is derived from the word *chairō*, a verb translated "to rejoice, be glad." The first definition of *charis* in Strong's concordance is "that which affords joy, pleasure, delight." Grace and happiness are directly related, and they both stand in stark opposition to bitterness and trouble. A man or woman of grace bears a heart free from bitterness, just as a life of happiness includes a mind free from trouble.

Grace, however, can be impossible to conjure on our own. We must first receive the gift of grace from God in order to share it with others. Both Peter and James echo the proverb that says, "God is opposed to the proud, but gives grace to the humble" (James 4:6; 1 Peter 5:5; see also Proverbs 3:34).

This is a key to receiving and then expressing grace. Those who lack grace tend to exude pride as well as bitterness. If we are to receive God's grace, we can either humble ourselves before the Lord or wait until our circumstances humble us.

I met a well-known television evangelist several times when I was a child. Behind the scenes, he was arrogant and somewhat rude. Then a scandal humiliated him. Years later, I met him again, but this time I was an adult. He was a completely different man, full of grace and devoid of pride. I remember people bemoaning the scandal at the time, asking why God would allow such a thing to happen to a prominent Christian leader. But anyone who knew him before and after the fall understood. God humbled him in order to give him grace. This is one of the definitions of happiness—literally. The Hebrew verb *yatab*, often translated as "to be good, pleasing, or glad," can also be translated, "to make a thing good or right or beautiful." Humility that leads to grace transforms a bitter, arrogant life, making it beautiful.

Rooting Out Bitterness

Whatever the cause of bitterness, it must be eradicated to make room for joy. The effects of bitterness cause trouble and defile many, as Hebrews tells us. Though others may see the outward symptoms of a bitter heart, each of us must deal honestly and introspectively to face the inner truth.

We must drink freely of the grace of God and humbly admit our own weakness. When Paul faced his "thorn in the flesh," the Lord told him, "My grace is sufficient for you, for power is perfected in weakness" (2 Corinthians 12:7,9). God's grace is enough, but we must diligently seek it. He is faithful to complete His work in us when we turn over our lives completely to Him.

4

PRIDE

*"Man," I cried, "how ignorant art
thou in thy pride of wisdom!"*

MARY SHELLEY, *FRANKENSTEIN*

K ing Xerxes was one of the most powerful kings of the Old Testament. After months of feasting and celebrating with his people through-out his vast kingdom, he honored a man named Haman and "established his authority over all the princes who were with him" (Esther 3:1).

As the newly promoted Haman left the banquet, everyone bowed down to him except for one man. Mordecai was a Jew and the cousin of a young woman who had recently been made queen, Hadassah, also known as Esther. A short time later, Haman was invited to a series of private banquets with the king and queen, an unparalleled honor for such a man. As he left the first banquet, he passed by Mordecai, who again refused to bow down to a man. The book of Esther recounts it this way: "Then Haman went out that day glad [*sameach*] and pleased [*towb*] of heart; but when Haman saw Mordecai in the king's gate and that he did not stand up or tremble before him, Haman was filled with anger against Mordecai" (Esther 5:9).

Here was a man whose life was on the fast track for success. He had power, position, wealth, and favor. But he also had pride. He was doubly happy that day until his pride caused him to be angry. Then his happiness evaporated, and in his rage, he conspired to kill not only Mordecai but also every other Jew in the kingdom. He didn't know that Queen Esther was also a Jew, and his actions eventually backfired, leading to not only his own brutal death by impalement but also the same fate for his ten sons.

And who was Mordecai to Haman? Nobody. He was just an old man hanging around the king's gate. If Haman had just dismissed him, Haman might have had a long life. Mordecai meant no offense to Haman; he was merely living by his personal religious convictions. He wasn't defying Haman, protesting the king's promotion of him, or stirring up rancor against either of them. He merely stood. But Haman took offense—in fact, he reached out and grabbed it. He let it define his mood and eventually his actions. His pride allowed one man's benign posture to become his downfall and destruction. Haman graphically illustrates the truth that "pride goes before destruction, and a haughty spirit before stumbling" (Proverbs 16:18).

Before his ultimate destruction, Haman missed what could have been a wake-up call. We've seen that Haman left the banquet "glad" and "pleased." He was happy. But then he saw Mordecai. His pride was offended, his joy evaporated, and anger took control.

Moody people—those who swing from happiness to anger in an instant—are frequently controlled by pride. Their happiness disappears as soon as someone does something that displeases them. This is not the Christian life Jesus and His disciples described. Had Haman recognized this illogical mood swing in himself, he might have been able to diagnose his pride and avoid death.

When Paul wrote about the various parts of the body of Christ, he touched on the essence of pride. "For through the grace given to me I say to everyone among you not to think more highly of himself than he ought" (Romans 12:3). Note that he does not say that we should not think of ourselves at all. If we are to love our neighbors as ourselves as Jesus instructed, we must first love ourselves. The sin of pride is a sin of excess—loving ourselves more than we should.

Pride caused Lucifer to believe he could supplant God. He had been given great gifts but not as great as he thought. This excess perverts things that would otherwise be good or at least innocuous.

Consider these expressions of pride:

Pride Wants Everyone's Attention

Good communication requires that we hold someone's attention. Many of the gifts of the Spirit incorporate an ability to command a crowd. Jesus was often the center of attention, as were Paul and Silas as they spread the gospel. But when people feel an overwhelming desire for others to notice their abilities, watch their performance, or hear their opinions, pride has taken root.

Paul wrote, "May it never be that I would boast, except in the cross of our Lord Jesus Christ" (Galatians 6:14). Demanding attention for our gifts, accomplishments, and ideas puts us between the crowd and the cross. That's a foolish and dangerous place to be.

Pride Is Always Right

I don't know anyone who tries to be wrong. Most normal people try to figure out what is right and live by it. When we make a decision or argue a position, we typically do so because we think it is best. Even so, most people will admit they are sometimes wrong. Pride, however, makes excuses, justifies its wrongness, or doubles down on the ill-fated position. When pride can't deny its mistake, it will often shift the blame elsewhere. "I was wrong, but…" or "I am sorry it happened, but…" or the classic "I am sorry if you were offended," as if the problem lies in the recipient, not the one who committed the wrongdoing—these communicate no real apology and no genuine contrition.

The most memorable character on the sitcom *Happy Days* was Henry Winkler's Fonzie. He was the classic rebel without a cause. He wore a leather jacket, drove a motorcycle, and couldn't get past the *s* in *I'm sorry*. If he tried to say, "I was wrong," he would get to the *w*, and his mouth would refuse to function. It was great for laughs, but it's not funny when real people live in that kind of world. We must recognize our imperfections and humbly admit when we are wrong.

Pride Strives to Impress People

Again, few people set out to make a bad impression on others. We should have good manners, groom ourselves, and generally try to be pleasant. But when one constantly works to elicit flattery, that's pride. (Insecurity can also do this, but that's generally for some kind of affirmation instead of vainglory.)

Prideful people will often flatter others for their own gain. Jude wrote about people who "speak arrogantly, flattering people for the sake of gaining an advantage" (Jude 1:16). Arrogance and pride love an atmosphere of empty flattery. It puffs the ego and perpetuates the illusion.

Solomon put flattery and happiness on opposite sides. "A man who flatters his neighbor is spreading a net for his steps. By transgression an evil man is ensnared, but the righteous sings [*ranan*] and rejoices [*samach*]" (Proverbs 29:5-6). An excessive desire to impress, flatter, and receive praise is a snare, and genuine joy is its victim.

Pride Has to Stay One Step Ahead

Keeping up with the Joneses is nothing but pride in motion. Having a nice house is fine unless you buy it to show up someone else. If your coworker buys a new car and you feel as if you have to buy a nicer one, that's pride.

"For all that is in the world, the lust of the flesh and the lust of the eyes and the boastful pride of life, is not from the Father, but is from the world" (1 John 2:16). The Greek word for *pride* is *alazoneia*. It means "empty, braggart talk." It is defined as "an insolent and empty assurance that trusts in its own power and resources and shamefully despises and violates divine laws and human rights."

This type of pride is especially ugly in religious circles. If the Presbyterian church in town builds a new auditorium and the Baptists and Methodists begin planning bigger auditoriums in response, they violate the divine laws of God. We must learn to be content to live in obedience, whatever shape or size that takes.

Pride Demands Its Rights

Certainly, we should stand up for the abused and oppressed. But when this crosses the line to demand unwarranted respect, entitlements, power, and position, it's nothing but pride. The civil rights movement in America expressed a righteous call for justice and equality. But out of that, some have taken a position of exploitation and opportunism. Martin Luther King Jr. never wavered on his position, yet he walked in humility. He never sought to take his "pound of flesh," to quote Shakespeare, but merely asked for America to live up to its ideals.

Now, it seems that anything that someone wants is a right. If a mother wants to terminate the life in her womb, it is a "woman's right." If two men want to rewrite the traditions of civilization to consecrate their relationship, it is called "gay rights." Government workers claim a right to extract demands from the tax-paying public. When rights become wrongs, they cease to have moral validity. Laying down our pride and seeking to serve others in love accomplishes far more than making vain demands on society.

Pride Can't Take Losing

Nobody sets out to lose, whether in a sporting event, sales contest, political race, or any other form of competitive endeavor. But defeat should motivate us to perform better; it should not cause anger, envy, or hatred. Even when we are cheated, we must overcome evil with good.

Paul tells us that love "is not provoked" and "does not take into account a wrong suffered" (1 Corinthians 13:5). It's difficult to not get upset when others get ahead wrongly. Only with patience, forgiveness, and security in our identity in Christ can we move beyond it. Pride will keep you stuck in bitter defeat.

On one side, there is love and happiness. On the other, pride and discontent. Which side are you on? Do you seek praise and glory? Do you celebrate others' success or envy their accomplishments? Are you angered by those who don't give you the respect you are due? Do you brag about yourself, or can you say, as the psalmist did, "My soul will make its boast in the LORD; the humble will hear it and rejoice [*samach*]" (Psalm 34:2)?

G.K. Chesterton quipped, "Pride is a poison so very poisonous that it not only poisons the virtues; it even poisons the other vices." If you have pride in your life, you will find it very difficult to experience happiness. Pride will poison your ability to experience love, peace, patience, and every other fruit of the Spirit, including joy.

Poor in Spirit

In the Sermon on the Mount, Jesus taught, "Blessed are the poor in spirit, for theirs is the kingdom of heaven" (Matthew 5:3).

This surprising statement seems to speak against education, intellectualism, and ability. But Jesus was taking a shot at those who prided themselves in their own abilities, and He was giving hope to those considered to be lower-class. He was saying that when we realize our deficiency and confess our need for the Holy Spirit, we find God's kingdom riches.

The poor in spirit admit their shortcomings and open themselves up to God's grace. The proud, however, believe that they can earn righteousness through their own learning, effort, and status. Pride takes credit for things that God has accomplished, but the poor in spirit know that nothing good comes to us except from Jesus Christ. Realizing that we are spiritually weak on our own allows us to be filled with His strength.

TAKING OFFENSE

*Pride and jealousy there was in his eye, for
his life had been spent in asserting rights
which were constantly liable to invasion.*

SIR WALTER SCOTT, *IVANHOE*

C ody Goodnight walked into a Family Dollar store in east Fort Worth
to buy a couple of sodas for his five-year-old son and himself. The
clerk, Ricky Young, had some difficulty with the scanner and attempted
to make small talk while handling the register. Cody did not respond.

Once the sodas rang up, Cody paid in cash. Ricky felt insulted for
being ignored, so he threw the change at Cody, scattering it on the floor.
The 31-year-old father bent down to pick it up and at that point, Ricky
later told police, muttered a racial slur and threatened him. So Ricky
picked up a crowbar from behind the register and clubbed the man
behind the ear.

Cody stumbled out of the store without a word, went home, and
reported the incident to his mother. She and her husband contacted the
police. When officers arrived at the discount store, Ricky was still working.

They checked the surveillance video, but it had mysteriously been erased. They took Ricky's statement claiming racism and self-defense and then informed him of one significant fact.

Cody Goodnight was deaf.

When Cody was a toddler, a high fever robbed him of his ability to hear. He can make guttural noises but tries to remain silent because people have made fun of him. He communicates through sign language.

"When you're deaf, you don't make a point of starting conversations with people," Cody's mother said. Yet at least one person took offense at this deaf man's behavior, misconstruing it for disrespect.

We live in an offensive world. It tempts us every day. Taking offense often seems justifiable, but it is never good. It becomes a major obstacle to happiness if we are not conscious of it or fail to understand the biblical remedies for it.

Offense comes at us in four ways.

Intentional Offense

You would have to live alone on an island to not run across someone who wants to irritate you. Drivers flash crude gestures when you drive too fast or too slow. Sports fans hurl profanity if you wear the wrong colors at a game. The emergence of online interaction has made offensive communication exponentially easier. And these are just the surface annoyances. Coworkers sometimes tear down others to elevate themselves. Siblings can be brutal to one another. Couples learn how to push each other's buttons to get a negative reaction. Offense is an unfortunate reality of this world.

The Bible tells us not to intentionally give offense (1 Corinthians 10:32) or receive it (1 Corinthians 13:5). This is not easy. Human nature wants offenders to "get what they deserve." If payback comes at our own hand, the perverse satisfaction can be all the sweeter. If someone purposely offends you, the carnal reaction is to reciprocate with a greater offense. This is a bitter trap, diametrically opposed to Jesus' declaration that Christians should "rejoice [*chairō*] and be glad [*agalliaō*]" when persecuted by the world (Matthew 5:11-12).

If we should be happy when rejecting offense, we cannot possibly be anything but unhappy when we take it. "Never pay back evil for evil to anyone," Paul wrote in Romans 12:17. The practical problem with the endless circle of offense is that it ultimately leads to anger, violence, divorce, and all sorts of destructive behavior. It's a pit that we dig deeper with each returned insult or injury. If we ever want healing and restoration in relationships, we must learn to heed Paul's advice: "Be kind to one another, tender-hearted, forgiving each other, just as God in Christ also has forgiven you" (Ephesians 4:32).

Unintended Offense

People who offend others most often don't intend to. Nonetheless, the miscommunication can quickly lead to confusion, pent-up anger, and division. Once, when about to leave for a family gathering, I noticed my wife had dressed more formally than the occasion required. In my ill-timed attempt to let her know that she could be more casual and, in my mind, more comfortable, I said, "You don't need to dress up so much."

I thought I was doing her a favor. I was wrong! She heard something more along the lines of, "All your effort to look nice is a waste of time." She was, of course, offended and upset, which left me completely confused. She thought I was being rude, but I thought I was being considerate. I let her reaction irritate me, and we departed late and unhappy. I have since learned to either inform her of the appropriate attire well ahead of time or keep my mouth shut. Better yet, I can tell her how great she looks!

Similar scenarios are played out every day. Some people are quicker to interpret things as offensive than other people are, so if we are to avoid such conflict, we need to consider our words carefully and communicate our meaning clearly. To avoid being easily offended ourselves, we must learn to do two things. First, we need to give people the benefit of the doubt. Don't assume that people are trying to be offensive. Let them be explicit in their offense before judging their words and actions. Second, develop a supernatural habit of forgiveness and grace. The New Living Translation says it best: "Make allowance for each other's faults, and forgive anyone who offends you" (Colossians 3:13).

Be warned: You cannot do this on your own. You may be able to grin and bear it for a while, but enduring grace and forgiveness come only through a close relationship with Jesus Christ and a practiced attitude of humility and patience. But if you learn how to purge unintended offenses from your life—neither offending others nor taking offense—you will be happier, and so will the people around you.

Imagined or Misperceived Offenses

Some people seem to be looking for offense, as was the Family Dollar clerk. They take it when it is not theirs to take. Sadly, a perverse sort of American industry goads people to find offense and react to it. Politicians, activists, shock jocks, and others exploit divisions and exacerbate offenses. People are sometimes taught that people of a different race, gender, or sexual orientation are out to offend them.

This is perhaps the most insidious and even demonic form of offense. It feeds on stereotypes, past grievances, and fiction. Christians must never succumb to such foolishness. Perhaps the most noticeable example of Christians falling into this trap occurs during what should be one of the most reverent and happy occasions of the year: Christmastime.

I have heard people on talk radio complain that store clerks have said, "Happy holidays" instead of "Merry Christmas." This surely must have been an intentional slap at Christianity, the callers insist. What nonsense. And even if someone avoids uttering the word *Christmas*, who cares? Regardless of what someone says, we can always return a warm smile and hearty "Merry Christmas!"

People who go looking for offense are usually miserable. Happiness is completely incompatible with this foolish and dangerous mind-set. Christians should not give in to the temptation to play the social martyr. We should stand up for our beliefs and defend assaults on our faith but never look for reasons to take offense. To the contrary, we must proactively forgive those who offend us whether the offense is real or merely perceived. Otherwise, we play the part of the angry, bitter, unhappy victim.

Offended by God

This can happen to any of us, but carnal, selfish, or evil people will almost certainly be offended by God. Jesus said, "Blessed is he who does not take offense at Me" (Luke 7:23). The people in the New Testament who repeatedly took offense at Jesus were the religious leaders. Why were they offended? Indeed, why is anyone offended by Jesus, regardless of whether he or she is religious?

Two simple reasons stand out. First, we are offended by God because He does not behave as we wish. The Pharisees were offended that Jesus Christ claimed to be the Promised One. They didn't believe the Messiah would look like Jesus.

> When the Sabbath came, He began to teach in the synagogue; and the many listeners were astonished, saying, "Where did this man get these things, and what is this wisdom given to Him, and such miracles as these performed by His hands? Is not this the carpenter, the son of Mary, and brother of James and Joses and Judas and Simon? Are not His sisters here with us?" And they took offense at Him (Mark 6:2-3).

The religious leaders wanted a king. They wanted someone who would punish the Romans for their cruelty. They recognized Jesus' wisdom and miracles, but He didn't fit the full profile of their concept of the Messiah. Throughout history, God has not fit the profile of man's expectations. People want a god who allows no suffering, a god who dispenses justice only on their terms, a god who loves sin as much as the sinner, a god who looks like them. This has caused great offense.

Even believers can take offense at God when He does not behave as we wish. We pray for healing, but someone dies. We tithe faithfully but fall into debt. We seek reconciliation with someone but are rejected. We may *take* offense in these circumstances (God does not give it), and when we do, the result can be bitterness and a hardness of heart. We must be careful to avoid the easy offense. Instead, we can push closer to God for comfort and understanding.

Second, some people take offense at the very idea that God exists. Atheists elevate their own minds to a humanly impossible position, supposedly knowing beyond doubt that a Creator does not exist, so the suggestion of God offends their enormous pride.

Rejecting all forms of offense is the mark of wisdom and spiritual maturity. "A person's wisdom yields patience; it is to one's glory to overlook an offense" (Proverbs 19:11 NIV). If we are to rise above the sins of this world and find true happiness, we must move beyond giving or taking offense.

Victimhood

Dennis Prager, a Jewish scholar and radio talk-show host, believes that one of the greatest obstacles to happiness is an attitude of victimhood. He points out that people with a victim mentality feel as if their lives are determined by others. He says that this belief leads to anger, an addiction to self-pity, and an unhealthy craving for sympathy—all of which render happiness impossible.

"In our time," Prager wrote in his book *Happiness Is a Serious Problem*, "the problem of regarding oneself primarily as a victim is not, ironically, so much a problem among actual victims... as it is among people who have decided to see themselves as victims."

Dr. A.R. Bernard, pastor of the largest church in New York City and a brilliant thinker, wrote this in his book *Happiness Is...*

> It's amazing how many people, especially those who portray themselves as "victims," conclude that the lives they're experiencing have been chosen for them. But they're mistaken. In truth, their lives—all of our lives—are composed of our choices...and we become servants to the choices we make.

God does not intend for us to be emotional slaves to our circumstances. He expects us to consciously choose the right response to every situation and trust Him to cause "all things to work together for good to those who love God, to those who are called according to His purpose" (Romans 8:28).

Adopting an attitude of victimhood causes a person to take offense at virtually everything. It is slavery. In Christ, we must know the truth in order to be free. And the truth is that we are not victims; we are overcomers.

6

EXPECTATIONS

*I'm afraid to do what I want to do. Always
thinking of the family dignity. I haven't
taken a free step for twenty-five years.*

P.G. WODEHOUSE, *A DAMSEL IN DISTRESS*

Jesus Christ was a failure. Many religious leaders and experts of the Old Testament law expected a Messiah who would cast off the oppression of the Romans and establish an earthly kingdom. Instead, Jesus spoke of an invisible kingdom and died on a cross like a common criminal. He was, in the view of many, a major disappointment.

Such is the problem with expectations.

When we are caught in the trap of unfulfilled expectations, we are unable to be happy. Such notions can come from others or be self-imposed. Likewise, the expectations we place on other people can spread disappointment, anger, and strife.

Of course, Jesus was not a failure in God's eyes; He simply failed to meet the expectations of men. This is the first realization we must experience on our path to happiness. Nobody should attempt to live exclusively by other people's expectations. Ultimately, we answer only to God. This does not mean that God will not place people in our lives to encourage right living, provide a level of accountability, impart wisdom, and set certain standards. Parents do that for children. Employers do that for workers. Even pastors do that for their members. These should be taken into consideration, but they should not become hard rules by which we live. Every standard of man must be measured against the standards of God and the individual calling on our lives.

"Truly, truly, I say to you," Jesus said to the religious leaders who accused Him of blasphemy, "the Son can do nothing of Himself, unless it is something He sees the Father doing; for whatever the Father does, these things the Son also does in like manner" (John 5:19).

This was the standard for Jesus Christ. Certainly, this satisfied the expectations of some people, but it shattered the ideas of others. They weren't merely disappointed; they were offended. This will always be the case with man's expectations. They will vary so much that some people will be satisfied while other people are disappointed. This is an impossible game to play, and we should avoid it.

Jesus' expectations for His followers can be summed up in one verse: "If you love Me, you will keep My commandments" (John 14:15).

Granted, it can be argued that this is an impossible task, but it should be noted that He didn't add "all the time without fail." He knows that we will fail. That's why in the next verse Jesus said, "I will ask the Father, and He will give you another Helper, that He may be with you forever."

We have the Holy Spirit to help us fulfill Christ's commandments. This is the standard by which we live—God's expectations, not man's. Paul addressed this in his letter to the church in Galatia: "For am I now seeking the favor of men, or of God? Or am I striving to please men? If I were still trying to please men, I would not be a bond-servant of Christ" (Galatians 1:10).

When we allow the Helper to guide us in our quest to fulfill Christ's expectations, God promises that we will bear fruit, including joy. If you are unhappy because other people do not approve of your life, determine whether you are striving for the favor of man or of God. If we are to serve Jesus Christ, we must cast off the ungodly expectations of others.

Aspirations

Another source of unhappiness can be the unfulfilled expectations we place on ourselves. Of these, there are two types: legitimate and illegitimate.

The son of a prominent Christian leader was once mistaken for his father. As he relates the story, he told the confused woman, "If you've seen the son, you've seen the father!" I was stunned and saddened when I heard this. As the son of a well-known evangelist, I would never aspire to be my father. That's not a negative or derogatory statement. He has achieved many great and wonderful things, but he did it by striving to be the man God wants him to be. As his son, I must seek to be the man God wants me to be, which is not the same as being the man God called my father to be. In fact, our personalities and gifts are so different that if I tried to be like him, I would be a complete fraud. I can only be myself, yielded to God so He can shape me into the unique person He created me to be.

This family dynamic is not exclusive to ministry. It can be seen in business, entertainment, politics, and virtually every vocation. Most children who strive to fill their parents' shoes are unhappy adults regardless of whether they succeed or fail. That's not to say that people cannot follow in their parents' line of work or ministry, but the children must operate as God directs and not try to repeat the life of someone else. Joel Osteen is a great example of a son who found his own calling even while stepping into his father's role. He didn't try to remake himself in his earthly father's image, but built on his father's legacy by hearing our heavenly Father for himself.

Ungodly self-expectations can never satisfy. If we fail to meet them, we are unhappy with no consolation. If we achieve things that are outside of God's design, we tend to be proud or self-righteous. Neither brings true joy or lasting happiness. The only legitimate aspiration is the desire to be the men or women God created us to be. Even when this is a struggle, it brings more peace and joy than any other aspiration.

Comparisons

Perhaps the most common tendency is to set our expectations according to the normal standards of our culture. For example, if everyone in our circle of influence drives a certain class of car or vacations in exotic locations, we feel the pressure to live up to that standard. This can also carry beyond material possessions. Parents can place undue pressure on their children to perform scholastically or athletically to keep up with other families. It can even creep into the church through spiritual one-upmanship. All of this is foolish and carnal. Paul wrote, "When they measure themselves by themselves and compare themselves with themselves, they are without understanding" (2 Corinthians 10:12).

My oldest daughter is an amazingly gifted artist. Her oil paintings have won statewide recognition in Texas. She is a member of the National Art Honor Society. My youngest daughter may have even more talent. Her photography shows an instinct for composition and perspective that nobody taught her. My oldest son has various works that are above average for someone his age. And then there's my youngest son.

It's not that his artwork is just inferior to the others'. By any standard, it's bad—laughably so. When the others draw detailed human figures with proper proportion and recognizable faces, he draws stick figures with enormous heads and warped features. Clearly, art is not his gift. If my wife and I dared to make his siblings' artistic abilities the standard for him, we would not only be unfair, we'd be cruel. Fortunately, while we all laugh at his attempts, we encourage him in other ways and openly admit that his talents lie elsewhere. Because we do not hold him to the same standard and compare him to the others, he is not insecure. He laughs too, and we are able to build him up in the talents God has obviously given him.

There will always be someone richer, smarter, more popular, more respected, more artistic, and so on. Conversely, there will always be someone poorer, less academic, less known, less respected, and so on. We are different by design. We have different gifts. We are given varying amounts of responsibility, creativity, visibility, wealth, and every other measure of man. Any attempt to equalize or compete in these arenas ignores God's true calling on our lives. It is foolish and futile. Avoid comparing yourself and your loved ones to others and focus on pursuing God's perfect will.

Ambition

Another illegitimate expectation we can place on ourselves is an ungodly ambition. From the Tower of Babel to the Garden of Gethsemane, the Bible is full of stories about man's plans gone awry. Anytime we seek things for ourselves that are outside of God's perfect plan for our lives—even things that seem noble or spiritual—we risk disappointment.

It has been speculated that Judas Iscariot was not out to betray Jesus, but to force Him to become the Messiah he had in mind. Regardless of whether that's the case, we know that even those closest to Christ sometimes confused God's plans with their own. Simon Peter cut off the ear of Malchus, a servant of the high priest who had come to seize Christ at Gethsemane, because Peter's plans were not in line with God's plan. Jesus was not unkind to Peter; He simply told him to put his sword back in his sheath. According to the Gospel of Luke, Jesus actually healed Malchus on the spot by reattaching his ear! Peter went on to deny Christ, as He predicted, but Jesus restored Simon Peter once again.

The pattern is clear. "There is a way which seems right to a man, but its end is the way of death" (Proverbs 14:12). We must learn to lay down our own ambitions and submit to the Lord. Jesus put it this way: "For whoever wishes to save his life will lose it, but whoever loses his life for My sake, he is the one who will save it" (Luke 9:24).

Our sole ambition must be obedience and submission to God's will, not our own. There isn't much happiness in death, but there is great joy in the resurrected life God promises to those who lay down their ambitions before the cross.

Condemnation

Perhaps the more difficult disappointments to overcome are the legitimate failures every person faces. Many of us are our own worst critics. We may legitimately strive to live by God's expectations and feel dejected or guilty when we fail. This can be the hardest roadblock to happiness to remove because the disappointment is often valid.

The critical facts to bear in mind are these: First, we all sin and fall short of God's glory (Romans 3:23). This is not an excuse to live in sin, but a statement of fact. We all miss the mark from time to time. The response God desires in these cases is not brooding over our failure or reveling in guilt, but repenting, turning from our errant ways, and pressing on toward Him (Philippians 3:14).

Second, God does not reveal our sin in order to pour guilt on us, but to show us a better way. "God did not send his Son into the world to condemn the world, but to save the world through him" (John 3:17 NIV). When we confess and repent, God offers forgiveness, restoration, peace, and joy. There is no condemnation in Him.

Third, we must learn the difference between essential and nonessential things. The Latin phrase *In necessariis unitas, in dubiis libertas, in omnibus caritas* rings true: In essentials, unity; in nonessentials, liberty; in all things, charity.

Paul addresses some of these things in Romans 14. He starts by saying, "Now accept the one who is weak in faith, but not for the purpose of passing judgment on his opinions" (verse 1). Then he discusses the differing views on eating meat, worshipping on a certain day of the week, and drinking wine. He reiterates certain absolute truths about Christ and then basically says two things about these other, nonessential issues: Don't judge each other, and don't force your views on others. He does not suggest that we compromise things we believe, but classifies some things as insignificant to the Christian life. "For the kingdom of God is not eating and drinking, but righteousness and peace and joy [*chara*] in the Holy Spirit" (verse 17). He neither condones nor justifies these different views, but says, "The faith which you have, have as your own conviction before God. Happy [*makarios*] is he who does not condemn himself in what he approves" (verse 22).

In short, we must strive to keep Jesus' commandments, repent when we know we're wrong, consider the opinions of others with measured grace, and avoid all forms of condemnation.

Our Expectations of Others

In addition to the expectations others place on us and those we place on ourselves are those we place on others. These can be delicate to navigate because part of our responsibility is to hold others accountable for certain things. As spouses, we expect our partners to work *with* us to achieve God's will, not against us. As parents, we are responsible to follow the wisdom of Proverbs 22:6: "Train up a child in the way he should go." As employers or supervisors, we are paid to insist people do their jobs properly. It's natural to be displeased when others fail or refuse to do what is right, but their performance should not rob us of our God-given joy.

We can learn a few things that will offset the potential for others' shortcomings to cause unhappiness. First, we can accept that others will make mistakes, disappoint us, and even purposely hurt us. That's why forgiveness is paramount to happiness. We shouldn't expect people to do wrong—that would be unwarranted pessimism—but we should not base our happiness on whether others meet our expectations.

In Peter's first letter, he wrote, "Love covers a multitude of sins" (4:8). The Greek word translated *sin* is *hamartia*, which can also be translated "to err or be mistaken." This doesn't mean that our love excuses, justifies, or accepts wrongdoing. It means that love is stronger. It's a simplistic analogy, but I tend to think of it like rock, paper, scissors. Just as paper covers rock, love covers sin. The sin is still there, but the love that God empowers in me keeps sin from stealing my joy.

We should also be realistic in our expectations of others. Our soul mates do not complete us; we are complete in Jesus Christ. Our children are not the source of our true joy; Jesus is. Careers do not fulfill us; pursuing God does. Acquiring material possessions does not enrich us; storing up treasures in God's kingdom does. All of these things—marriage, children, work, and wealth—can bring us pleasure, but they are not substitutes for the joy God gives us. These things will all pass away, but the things of the Lord will last forever (Matthew 24:35). We should appreciate when these lesser things work out in our favor, but we should also keep our hearts set on the greater things of God. When these expectations are properly aligned with kingdom purpose and power, they are not given undue influence over our lives.

Finally, we must learn to trust in God's sovereignty. We cannot see to the next day, but God sees beyond our individual lives. We expect certain things—long life, general well-being, reward for our work, and so on—but we are not in control. God is. Just as the Lord allows us to err in our ways, always maintaining the heart of the prodigal son's father, we should also endure the failed expectations of others. When we allow misery to preside because of the actions of others, we effectively choose to distrust God's wisdom and justice. We must, as the familiar prayer says, seek the serenity to accept the things we cannot change, the courage to change the things we can, and the wisdom to know the difference.

Self-Imposed Expectations

During the dot-com boom, I was given the task to hire a sales force for a start-up tech company. I had little sales experience and had never hired salesmen. Taking the advice of our CFO, I set out a specific formula for sales and put the expectations in a written document. I then presented it to prospective employees and allowed them to decide whether they believed they could meet the goals. My main concern was the character of those we hired. Skills can be taught and developed, but bad ethics, habits, and morals can be terribly difficult to overcome.

If the salesmen could meet the targeted numbers during their probationary period, they were guaranteed a job. If not, they agreed to be terminated. Nobody I interviewed believed they couldn't meet the goals. In hindsight, they weren't that difficult. But I noticed something quite interesting within a few months. The salesmen who managed their own expectations the best also performed the best.

One salesman became discouraged quickly. If a day went by without making a sale, his confidence sagged. After a particularly long dry spell, he simply became unable to perform. He didn't pursue good leads. He couldn't convince anyone to buy our product. He lost faith in himself because he failed to meet his own expectations. After six months, I didn't even have to fire him. When I presented his sales figures, he said, "Thanks for the opportunity," packed up his personal effects, and left.

Our best salesman, on the other hand, realized that his job was essentially a numbers game. A certain percentage of prospective buyers would come through, and some would require more persistence than others. He never got discouraged when someone rejected our offer. To him, it wasn't personal; it was just part of the process. He moved on to the next prospect and kept the sales cycle moving. He managed his expectations well, and as a result, he sold more than anyone else.

We often put undue pressure on ourselves. When we fail to meet our own expectations, we may become discouraged. These feelings can spiral downward into self-defeat. If our efforts to improve our marriage are met with resistance or disinterest, we quit trying. If we raise our children right but they make bad decisions, we question God's word. If we pray for something and it doesn't happen, we quit praying.

We seem to believe that in the end God will say, "Well done, good and perfect servant." But that's not the standard. Jesus' parable of the talents ended well for those to whom the master said, "Well done, good and *faithful* servant" (Matthew 25:21 NIV). We are not called to always succeed. We are called to be faithful.

We should also accept God's grace in our own lives. We can never outdo God in the grace department, so as we examine our ways and turn from any errant thoughts and behavior, we should also forgive ourselves, allow the Holy Spirit to comfort and encourage us, and seek to give our best in everything God entrusts to us.

Expectations, when treated as standards to which we aspire, benefit us. But when they become objects of discouragement or clubs with which we bludgeon ourselves and others, they are destructive. Managing them in light of God's word and character is essential to the joy we possess and impart to others.

7

UNFORGIVENESS

I could easily forgive his pride, if
he had not mortified mine.

JANE AUSTEN, *PRIDE AND PREJUDICE*

My worst college roommate is now one of my best friends. The first week of my freshman year at Oral Roberts University, I sat down in a class next to John. Next to him was Debbie, a girl he had grown up with in Florida. Over the course of our first semester, John and I became friends, and Debbie and I went out several times. Oral Roberts University does not have fraternities; it has wings, where guys live on the same hall, share the same restrooms, compete in intramural sports as a team, engage in social events together, and partner with a "sister wing" for dining, seating in chapel, and other coordinated activities. After our freshman year, John and I decided we would move to the same wing and room together.

At the beginning of our sophomore year, John casually asked me if Debbie and I would be dating again. She spent her summer in Florida while I spent mine in Texas. Though we communicated a few times, we were not serious, so it was a fair question. "Probably not," I answered, thinking of a few other girls I wanted to date.

I thought he was asking because we were all friends. I was wrong. I knew that they were spending some time together, going to the mall or the movies, but I had no idea he was hoping for a more serious relationship with her. They were childhood friends, so it was natural for them to do things together. It didn't last long because Debbie did not share his vision for their future, and nobody said anything to me about any of this. So when I ran into her on turkey tetrazzini night at the campus cafeteria, I didn't have a clue about the storm I would unleash.

In college, bad food was great for my dating life. If the menu was unpopular, all a guy had to do was hang around the entrance to the cafeteria and wait for girls' reactions. Find someone you were interested in, offer her dinner at a nearby restaurant, and a quick date was a sure thing. That's how Debbie and I ended up going to dinner one night. If I remember correctly, a movie followed.

When John heard this, he felt betrayed. I had lied to him! Of course, I didn't know I was making some sort of commitment months prior by answering his question. I also didn't know he had unsuccessfully courted her. But he had ample justification to think I had totally stabbed him in the back.

He didn't confront me directly. Instead, our relationship rapidly deteriorated. We were both young and immature, and naturally, we had other differences. Those small differences became big, and by the spring semester, John moved out. We had gone from being good friends to despising each other. It wasn't until the end of the school year that a mutual friend told me John's side of the story. Before leaving for the summer, I apologized, and John graciously accepted my apology. A few months later, during our junior year, our friendship resumed. Two years later, when Debbie and I got married, John stood by my side as a groomsman. Twenty years later, because of forgiveness, he and I are still great friends.

It's no secret that unforgiveness is a major obstacle to happiness. Even medical professionals understand its power. Katherine Piderman of the Mayo Clinic writes, "If you don't practice forgiveness, you may be the one who pays most dearly. By embracing forgiveness, you embrace peace, hope, gratitude and joy."

Examining forgiveness in our lives requires focusing on three equally important areas: forgiving ourselves, forgiving others, and forgiving God.

Forgiving Yourself

Certain personalities can be especially unforgiving of themselves. I know; I'm one of them. We can be our own worst enemies, beating ourselves up for failures long ago confessed. Many people spend endless time and energy trying to make up for their own shortcomings. Freedom begins when you realize that you will never be good enough for God. On your own merit, you will always fall short of the glory of God (Romans 3:23).

The good news is that God knows this and has made provision for it. This is the core part of Jesus' mission. At the Last Supper, He said, "This is My blood of the covenant, which is poured out for many for forgiveness of sins" (Matthew 26:28).

Peter preached this message in the first-century church as the gospel: "Of Him all the prophets bear witness that through His name everyone who believes in Him receives forgiveness of sins" (Acts 10:43).

Paul wrote it to the churches: "In Him we have redemption through His blood, the forgiveness of our trespasses, according to the riches of His grace which He lavished on us" (Ephesians 1:7-8).

John reiterated it to all believers: "If we confess our sins, He is faithful and righteous to forgive us our sins and to cleanse us from all unrighteousness" (1 John 1:9).

The psalmist even declared it before the birth of Christ: "As far as the east is from the west, so far has He removed our transgressions from us" (Psalm 103:12).

The reasons we indulge in self-unforgiveness are all wrong. Arrogance, deception, self-pity, unbelief…whatever it may be, it's siding with Satan, not God. That is why he is described as "the accuser of our brethren…who accuses them before our God day and night" (Revelation 12:10).

So when we can't forgive ourselves, the question becomes, why side with the devil? Jesus did not come to condemn us, but to freely offer forgiveness through His grace, which runs deeper than any of our sins. Of course, if you have not agreed with God that sin is sin and repented by turning from it daily, then that must first occur. But once that is done, it's done. Stop punishing yourself by believing the lie that your confessed sins have not been wiped clean!

"How blessed ['esher] is he whose transgression is forgiven, whose sin is covered! How blessed ['esher] is the man to whom the LORD does not impute iniquity, and in whose spirit there is no deceit!" (Psalm 32:1-2). The Hebrew word 'esher is a noun also translated as "happiness." To "impute iniquity" is to place value or accountability on wrongdoing. God's desire is to devalue our sin, making it worthless, and to give us happiness in return. If you are struggling in this area, start each day by declaring that you are forgiven. And when you do fail, confess again and move on. Only when you learn to forgive yourself can you move on to the next steps.

Forgiving Others

A father bought a bag of candy and put a handful into cups to share with his two young children. His son devoured the sweets, and while his sister was distracted, he took her cup and ate her candy too. When she noticed, she cried out, and the father realized what had happened. His son readily confessed, and seeing how upset his sister was, he said he was sorry. But she would have none of it. She had suffered an injustice, and she was rightfully angry.

"I have a whole bag of candy," the father said. "I will give you more, but you need to forgive your brother."

"No," she cried. "He took *mine*!"

"But I have more," the father repeated. "I will give you more than he took if you will accept his apology."

The little girl wouldn't budge. In her mind, the hurt and anger were justified, and she couldn't see past that. She would not forgive. Saddened, the father put the rest of the candy in the cupboard and left her to sulk.

This is the essence of unforgiveness. Obviously, the pain and injustice we suffer is far worse than a cupful of candy, but the principle is the same. Whatever mankind can take from us, God is able to restore many times over. Has someone stolen from you? God owns everything; He can give you more. Has someone robbed you of your peace? He can give you the peace that passes understanding. Has someone hurt your loved ones? God can restore them as well as you. Even the most painful offenses—divorce, disfigurement, rape, and even murder—are not beyond God's ability to restore and heal. Some things will not be made whole in this lifetime, but God promises comfort and the restoration of happiness if we will only forgive.

Jesus was not oblivious to the damage others can do to us. Nonetheless, when Peter asked, "Lord, how often shall my brother sin against me and I forgive him? Up to seven times?" Jesus answered, "I do not say to you, up to seven times, but up to seventy times seven" (Matthew 18:21-22).

In the Jewish culture, the number seven represents wholeness and completion. Jesus was not stating a hard number of 490 times; He was speaking of the wholeness that comes when we make forgiveness a way of life. Furthermore, He tied God's forgiveness for us to our forgiveness of others. "If you forgive others for their transgressions, your heavenly Father will also forgive you. But if you do not forgive others, then your Father will not forgive your transgressions" (Matthew 6:14-15). Paul restated this principle to the church when he wrote, "Just as the Lord forgave you, so also should you" (Colossians 3:13).

Even when others are not aware of their offenses, when they refuse to admit what they have done, or when they do not ask our forgiveness, we must let go. "For by your standard of measure it will be measured to you in return" (Luke 6:38).

The problem with unforgiveness is that it places us in God's judgment seat. If He forgives our sins and offers forgiveness to others, who are we to not do the same? For the believer, withholding forgiveness is not an option. Yet we easily deceive ourselves by ignoring or justifying our attitude. Churches are filled with people who hold grudges and harbor pain. That is one reason why individuals and even congregations fail to truly enter into worship. Jesus said, "If you are presenting your offering at the altar, and there remember that your brother has something against you, leave your offering there before the altar and go; first be reconciled to your brother, and then come and present your offering" (Matthew 5:23-24).

How many times have you sung songs of praise, given tithes and offerings, prayed for yourself or others, conducted a Bible study, or entered into any form of ministry while conveniently looking past the unforgiveness in your heart? This is a wall. Healing, reconciliation, peace, and joy lie on the other side, and forgiveness is the only hammer that can bring down the wall. It may not be easy, but for our own benefit, we are commanded to tear down the walls of unforgiveness.

On a practical level, I should point out that the concept of "forgive and forget" is not necessarily scriptural. Granted, this is what God offers us, but in order to exercise wisdom, we must learn even while we forgive.

For example, I have innocently done things that caused pain or anger in loved ones. I certainly did not intend harm, and I can honestly say that my heart was pure. In some cases, I believe the other person was wrong for quickly taking offense, especially over something not intended to be offensive. Still, we can do things that unintentionally hurt others. Asking for forgiveness (even when we feel like we shouldn't have to) demonstrates the character that the Holy Spirit wants to cultivate in us. The fruit of the Spirit typically described as patience, forbearance, or longsuffering empowers us to graciously endure and work through such things.

But in the process of giving or seeking forgiveness, we should not forget what we did that gave offense. Conversely, if someone repeatedly hurts us, it may be wise to disallow that person to be in a position to hurt us again. Sometimes, we must "shake the dust off our feet" and peacefully walk away rather than suffer continuous abuse. It is not always wise to remain in a position of giving or receiving offense in the anticipation of endless forgiveness. Dealing with complex situations requires wisdom and discernment on our part, but Paul's exhortation bears heeding. "If possible, so far as it depends on you, be at peace with all men" (Romans 12:18).

It has been said that bitterness is the poison we swallow in order to hurt others. Unforgiveness is the main ingredient in this poison. It defiles us first and foremost. If we are to find true happiness, we must learn to forgive others.

Forgiving God

We now come to the strange and illogical concept of holding a grudge against God. It may seem odd, but it is real. Often, it happens when we can't find anyone else to blame. An accident takes a loved one, a disease tortures our own body, or an injustice cannot be attributed to any particular person. We even call natural disasters "acts of God" as if all He does is wreak havoc on mankind!

A receiver for the Buffalo Bills football team once dropped a game-winning pass in the end zone and posted this message on his Twitter account: "I PRAISE YOU 24/7!!!!!! AND THIS HOW YOU DO ME!!!!!

YOU EXPECT ME TO LEARN FROM THIS??? HOW???!!! ILL NEVER FORGET THIS!! EVER!!! THX THO…"

This frivolous example of blaming God for bad things reveals the fundamental silliness of such a notion. Many helpful books have been written to deal in depth with the subject, but the answer ultimately comes down to the sovereignty of God. His wisdom and purpose trump any of our reasoning. The psalmist expressed this idea in several ways.

- "From His dwelling place He looks out on all the inhabitants of the earth, He who fashions the hearts of them all, He who understands all their works" (Psalm 33:14-15).

- "Know that the Lord Himself is God; it is He who has made us, and not we ourselves; we are His people and the sheep of His pasture" (Psalm 100:3).

- "Our God is in the heavens; He does whatever He pleases" (Psalm 115:3).

The prophet Isaiah expressed the basic difference between God and man when he voiced these words of God: "'My thoughts are not your thoughts, nor are your ways My ways,' declares the Lord. 'For as the heavens are higher than the earth, so are My ways higher than your ways and My thoughts than your thoughts'" (Isaiah 55:8-9).

A pastor friend of mine expressed this eloquently after his daughter was tragically killed by a drunk driver. He told me that he said to God, "I don't understand this, so I'm just going to trust You."

Too often, our reaction to tragedy is, "I don't understand this, so I'm just going to *blame* You." My friend chose the wise path as he lived out this proverb: "Trust in the Lord with all your heart and do not lean on your own understanding" (Proverbs 3:5). With this attitude, he has been blessed. He does not blame God, and through it all, he has found genuine joy.

This is critical to our perception of God. We live in a fallen world. Bad things happen. We will not be able to make sense of everything that occurs in this life. Blaming God for suffering only creates more suffering. He does not require our forgiveness, but we must never be tempted to presume God guilty for things we do not understand. He is good. He gives us peace in the midst of the storm. He is not our enemy; He is our joy.

PART 2

MIXED BLESSINGS

Obstacles will always inhibit our happiness. Bitterness, disobedience, pride, and the other hindrances we have discussed can only harm us. They can never be turned for good. Instead, they must be thrown aside.

Conversely, the path of salvation, hope, wisdom, and other gifts of God always move us closer to Him. As a by-product, we become happier.

But many things can work either way. They can increase our happiness or decrease it. They can even work both ways simultaneously. These are the mixed blessings. We must learn how to use them as forces for good.

8

MONEY

To be clever enough to get all that money,
one must be stupid enough to want it.

G.K. CHESTERTON, *THE WISDOM OF FATHER BROWN*

Despite what the world may tell you, money is not a path to happiness. It is frequently an obstacle, although it doesn't have to be. Whether one is rich or poor, the relationship between finances and happiness is the same for everyone. Some of the greediest people in the world possess little, and some possess a lot. Some of the most generous are quite wealthy, and some aren't. Granted, a comfortable income averts many natural hardships, but the biblical reality is that we can be happy regardless of financial status.

Scripture includes instances of some wealthy people who were godly, such as Joseph and King Solomon, as well as some who were evil, such as King Ahab and the rich man who begged for a drink of water from Lazarus in the afterlife. Conversely, some people with little or no money were godly, such as the widow whom Elisha helped in 2 Kings and Peter when he admitted to the lame man, "I do not possess silver and gold," and some were not, such as Job's wife after all his wealth was gone.

Money is not a measure of godliness, nor is it the determining factor when it comes to happiness. "Better [*towb*] is the little of the righteous than the abundance of many wicked" (Psalm 37:16).

There are three money-related issues that determine whether it is an obstacle to our happiness.

Attitude

My father likes to say, "It's okay to have possessions as long as they don't possess you." This truth is illustrated in the story of the rich young ruler, who was trying to work his way into heaven. Jesus told him, "If you wish to be complete, go and sell your possessions and give to the poor, and you will have treasure in heaven; and come, follow Me" (Matthew 19:21).

The man was not willing to part with his possessions, so "he went away grieving" (verse 22). Other translations use the words *sad* or *sorrowful*. Interestingly, the Greek word is not an adjective, but the verb *lypeō*, which means "to affect with sadness, to cause grief, to throw into sorrow." I think it's fair to say that the rich young ruler, who loved his money more than he loved Christ, caused his own unhappiness with his attitude.

Anytime the pursuit of money takes precedence over the pursuit of God, we are destined to be unhappy. "He who loves money will not be satisfied with money, nor he who loves abundance with its income" (Ecclesiastes 5:10).

The most famous but often misquoted passage about money tells us, "The love of money is a root of all sorts of evil, and some by longing for it have wandered away from the faith and pierced themselves with many griefs" (1 Timothy 6:10). It's not the money that causes evil or brings grief, it's the love of it—the attitude. When we love money, we inflict misery upon ourselves.

Instead, we must learn to be happy with little money or an abundance of wealth, as Paul stated in Philippians 4:11-12. Jesus pointedly tells us not to worry about the provisions that money provides.

> Do not worry then, saying, "What will we eat?" or "What will we drink?" or "What will we wear for clothing?" For the Gentiles eagerly seek all these things; for your heavenly Father knows that you need all these things. But seek first His kingdom and His righteousness, and all these things will be added to you (Matthew 6:31-33).

If your attitude is in line with God's will for your life, you may be rich or you may be poor, but either way, you can be happy.

Acquisition

The way we acquire money also affects our happiness. Proverbs 10:2 tells us, "Ill-gotten gains do not profit, but righteousness delivers from death." Making money unfairly or immorally impedes our happiness.

Jesus was passing through Jericho when He came across a rich man named Zaccheus. He was the chief tax collector in town, which basically meant he was crooked. He made much of his money by cheating, lying, and taking bribes. Jesus asked to stay at his house, and Zaccheus gladly agreed, but before they could even walk to his home, Zaccheus was convicted of his dishonest wealth. "Behold, Lord, half of my possessions I will give to the poor, and if I have defrauded anyone of anything, I will give back four times as much," Zaccheus declared (Luke 19:8).

Jesus responded, "Today salvation has come to this house." In Jesus' presence, we will realize the burden of our ill-gotten gain.

Scripture actually ties happiness with hard, honest work. "When you shall eat of the fruit of your hands, you will be happy [*'esher*] and it will be well [*towb*] with you" (Psalm 128:2). Integrity in our business dealings and efforts brings satisfaction and happiness, which are more valuable than a fat bank account. Moses even warned employers not to mistreat their workers: "Do not take advantage of a hired worker who is poor and needy" (Deuteronomy 24:14 NIV). Treating people fairly is another part of honest gain.

Administration

The third marker in our relationship with money is what we do with it. You only need to look at many of the young athletes, actors, pop stars, and other celebrities who suddenly come into large sums of money to see the havoc it can wreak in their lives. Billions of dollars have been wasted by people without the maturity and wisdom to properly handle it. In fact, money often fuels their early demise, whereas years of hard work and struggle can teach valuable lessons in money management.

There are many lessons in the Bible related to money—everything from investing it wisely (Matthew 25:14-23) to helping the cause of Christ (Mark

12:41-44; 2 Corinthians 8:1-7) to aiding the poor (Deuteronomy 14:28-29; Leviticus 23:22). We won't dive into a full study on financial administration, but notice that what we do with what God entrusts to us directly impacts our joy. It also can bring happiness to others, especially those in need.

My pastor, Bill Ramsey Jr., tells a great story about acquiring money. When he was a boy, his older sister taught him how to play the board game Monopoly. After repeatedly losing, the day finally came when the fortunes tilted in his favor. He acquired numerous properties, built houses and hotels, and amassed a sizeable stack of play money. Then, at the height of his excitement and success, his sister devastated him with two short words. "Game over," she said, and promptly folded the board and dumped everything back in the box. He was crushed. All of his success and wealth was gone in an instant. That, my pastor says, is exactly how life is. In the end, it all goes back in the box.

Everyone enters this world broke and goes out penniless. The real question isn't how much you will acquire in the interim, but what you will do with what you have. Ultimately, money can't bring happiness, but the proper attitude, acquisition, and administration of it can bless us and enable us to bless others.

Prosperity

Prosperity is a biblical concept, but it is often misunderstood and frequently abused. By examining the original words and context of the idea, we can begin to get a better picture of the true meaning.

Many times the Hebrew adjective *towb* is translated as *prosperous* or *prosperity*. It typically means "good, pleasant, agreeable, or beneficial."

- "See, I have set before you today life and prosperity [*towb*], and death and adversity" (Deuteronomy 30:15).
- "[The man who fears the LORD] will abide in prosperity [*towb*], and his descendants will inherit the land" (Psalm 25:13).
- "Adversity pursues sinners, but the righteous will be rewarded with prosperity [*towb*]" (Proverbs 13:21).
- "Thus says the LORD of hosts, 'My cities will again overflow with prosperity [*towb*], and the LORD will again comfort Zion and again choose Jerusalem'" (Zechariah 1:17).

All of these passages contrast the qualities of godly and ungodly men. The opposite of prosperity is not poverty but adversity. This is not to say that poverty is a blessing of God, but just to point out that the original word for prosperity in these passages is not necessarily related to wealth. However, it *is* directly related to happiness.

Also used is the proper noun *Towb Adoniyahuw*. He was one of the Levites sent by King Jehoshaphat to teach the law to the people throughout the cities of Judah. This is an interesting use of the phrase because it does not always refer to the person. His travels occurred about 912 BC, so the references in books written hundreds of years later appear to be personifications of goodness as brought by the word of God. Literally, the name means "my Lord is good." Again, it is placed in contrast to adversity.

- "The LORD will make you abound in prosperity [*Towb Adoniyahuw*], in the offspring of your body and in the offspring of your beast and in the produce of your ground, in the land which the LORD swore to your fathers to give you" (Deuteronomy 28:11).

- "Go and speak to Ebed-melech the Ethiopian, saying, 'Thus says the LORD of hosts, the God of Israel, "Behold, I am about to bring My words on this city for disaster and not for prosperity [*Towb Adoniyahuw*]; and they will take place before you on that day"'" (Jeremiah 39:16).

- "Visit me with Your salvation, that I may see the prosperity [*Towb Adoniyahuw*] of Your chosen ones, that I may rejoice in the gladness of Your nation, that I may glory with Your inheritance" (Psalm 106:4-5).

- "In the day of prosperity [*Towb Adoniyahuw*] be happy, but in the day of adversity consider—God has made the one as well as the other so that man will not discover anything that will be after him" (Ecclesiastes 7:14).

Another "happiness" word sometimes translated as *prosperity* is the verb *yatab*, which means "to be good, be pleasing, be well, be glad."

- "The LORD your God will bring you into the land which your fathers possessed, and you shall possess it; and He will prosper

> [*yatab*] you and multiply you more than your fathers" (Deuteronomy 30:5).

- "Jacob said, 'O God of my father Abraham and God of my father Isaac, O LORD, who said to me, "Return to your country and to your relatives, and I will prosper [*yatab*] you...""" (Genesis 32:9).

The noun *shalowm* is also used in a similar way. Often used as a greeting to mean "peace," it also denotes completeness, soundness, health, and contentment.

- "Let them shout for joy and rejoice, who favor my vindication; and let them say continually, 'The LORD be magnified, who delights in the prosperity [*shalowm*] of His servant'" (Psalm 35:27).

- "But the humble will inherit the land and will delight themselves in abundant prosperity [*shalowm*]" (Psalm 37:11).

- "For I was envious of the arrogant as I saw the prosperity [*shalowm*] of the wicked" (Psalm 73:3).

These uses of the word clearly point to prosperity as a spiritual and emotional condition. Wealth may be a part of God's blessing, but it's not the point. To use these passages to convey a purely monetary concept diminishes the original intent and distorts the true meaning.

However, some Hebrew words carry a more materialistic connotation and are often translated as prosperity. The verb *dashen* means "to grow fat, become prosperous." It is also used in the context of offerings to mean "to anoint" and "to take away ashes from the altar."

- "The generous man will be prosperous [*dashen*], and he who waters will himself be watered" (Proverbs 11:25).

- "An arrogant man stirs up strife, but he who trusts in the LORD will prosper [*dashen*]" (Proverbs 28:25).

- "The soul of the sluggard craves and gets nothing, but the soul of the diligent is made fat [*dashen*]" (Proverbs 13:4).

Note the path to material prosperity in these passages: generosity, humble trust, and diligence. Those who overemphasize material wealth typically don't advocate hard work as much as a bold (bordering on arrogant) shortcut. The concept of sowing a seed, as maligned as it may be, does have scriptural roots, but the biblical motivations are obedience, generosity, and trust, not greed, manipulation, or instant gratification.

Growth and progress are key components of prosperity. To gain does not specifically mean to get rich, but to improve in all things good and righteous. This is seen most pointedly in the verb *tsalach*, which means "to advance, prosper, make progress, succeed, or profit." This is the word most commonly translated *prosper*.

- "Then you will prosper [*tsalach*], if you are careful to observe the statutes and the ordinances which the LORD commanded Moses concerning Israel. Be strong and courageous, do not fear nor be dismayed" (1 Chronicles 22:13).

- "He said to Judah, 'Let us build these cities and surround them with walls and towers, gates and bars. The land is still ours because we have sought the LORD our God; we have sought Him, and He has given us rest on every side.' So they built and prospered [*tsalach*]" (2 Chronicles 14:7).

- "He continued to seek God in the days of Zechariah, who had understanding through the vision of God; and as long as he sought the LORD, God prospered [*tsalach*] him" (2 Chronicles 26:5).

- "'No weapon that is formed against you will prosper [*tsalach*]; and every tongue that accuses you in judgment you will condemn. This is the heritage of the servants of the LORD, and their vindication is from Me,' declares the LORD" (Isaiah 54:17).

- "He will be like a tree firmly planted by streams of water, which yields its fruit in its season and its leaf does not wither; and in whatever he does, he prospers [*tsalach*]" (Psalm 1:3).

- "Rest in the LORD and wait patiently for Him; do not fret because of him who prospers [*tsalach*] in his way, because of the man who carries out wicked schemes" (Psalm 37:7).

- "He who conceals his transgressions will not prosper [*tsalach*],

but he who confesses and forsakes them will find compassion"
(Proverbs 28:13).

- "Righteous are You, O LORD, that I would plead my case with
  You; indeed I would discuss matters of justice with You: Why
  has the way of the wicked prospered [*tsalach*]? Why are all
  those who deal in treachery at ease?" (Jeremiah 12:1).

It's interesting to note that the wicked also prosper. If only the righteous prospered, no evil men would be rich. But some evil men were rich
in the Old Testament, and the same is true today. In fact, some of the vil-
est displays of flesh and greed generate great sums of cash. Conversely,
some godly people lack wealth. Yet if we look at the spiritual condition
of both types, we will see who the truly prosperous ones are, regardless of
their economic condition.

The last Hebrew word often translated as *prosper* is the verb *sakal*. This
means "to be prudent, be circumspect, comprehend, or wisely understand." It specifically implies a more intellectual development. It is applied
to teachers and other wise men.

- "So keep the words of this covenant to do them, that you may
  prosper [*sakal*] in all that you do" (Deuteronomy 29:9).
- "David was prospering [*sakal*] in all his ways for the LORD was
  with him" (1 Samuel 18:14).
- "Behold, My servant will prosper [*sakal*], He will be high and
  lifted up and greatly exalted" (Isaiah 52:13).

Worldly prosperity is often foolish, but godly prosperity brings wisdom. This is a far more noble pursuit than wealth, and in fact, it will often
lead to an ability to acquire property and money. But the material aspect
is a temporary by-product of an eternal quality that ranks far higher in
importance than what we think of as being rich.

The Greek use of *prosperity* is much more sparse and basically encom-
passes three terms:

- *euporia*, a noun that means "riches, means, wealth"
- *euodoo*, a verb meaning "to lead by a direct and easy way, to
  be successful"

- *perisseuo*, a verb that generally means "to be left over, to overflow, to abound, or to exceed"

These are seen in a few passages in the New Testament:

- "These he gathered together with the workmen of similar trades, and said, 'Men, you know that our prosperity [*euporia*] depends upon this business'" (Acts 19:25).

- "On the first day of every week each one of you is to put aside and save, as he may prosper [*euodoo*], so that no collections be made when I come" (1 Corinthians 16:2).

- "Beloved, I pray that in all respects you may prosper [*euodoo*] and be in good health, just as your soul prospers [*euodoo*]" (3 John 1:2).

- "I know how to get along with humble means, and I also know how to live in prosperity [*perisseuo*]; in any and every circumstance I have learned the secret of being filled and going hungry, both of having abundance [*perisseuo*] and suffering need" (Philippians 4:12).

As is consistent with the Hebrew, the emphasis is placed on a spiritual, intellectual, and emotional sense of peace, wisdom, and improvement. The overarching point of prosperity is not financial gain, but a far deeper wealth of the soul and spirit.

On a purely observational level, the idea of material wealth is highly relative and subjective. If we measure one's faith by financial status, would we call Adam and Eve poor? Surely they prospered in the Garden of Eden, yet they had no money, no house, and no clothes. By today's standards, many of the richest people of the Old Testament would be poor. A rancher in Argentina may have hundreds of cattle, but his wealth pales in comparison to the stockbroker in New York City. Even America's poor, who often have televisions, air-conditioning, refrigeration, cell phones, and even cars, would be considered rich in every third-world nation.

Any organization that publicly works to feed hungry people on other continents, such as Africa, gets angry accusations from Americans of ignoring poverty here at home. Some people fail to grasp the difference between what sociologists call "relative poverty" and "abject poverty." In most Western countries, poor people are those in a certain lower percentage of the population. They may miss meals but rarely because no food exists in the community. America's homeless often go hungry on the same streets where all manner of exquisite food goes to waste in restaurants. This is not a lack of food, but a lack of distribution. But in the poorest countries of the world, there is no food to be found at all. At LIFE Outreach International, we have documented children literally eating dirt in an attempt to stave off hunger. *Relative poverty* describes those who are worse off financially than the majority of people in their country. *Abject poverty* means food, shelter, water, or other basic necessities cannot be found at all.

I am convinced that God is concerned with our abject poverty because He promises to supply all our needs according to His riches. He is clearly concerned with our spiritual poverty because He wants our souls to prosper. Material poverty ends when our basic needs are met. Anything above that is a level of prosperity for which we should be grateful, not dissatisfied.

Focusing on material wealth as a measure of prosperity means buying into the type of comparisons that the Bible expressly calls foolish. Instead, Christians should focus on the prosperity expressed in Proverbs 8:17-20.

> I love those who love me;
> And those who diligently seek me will find me.
> Riches and honor are with me,
> Enduring wealth and righteousness.
> My fruit is better than gold, even pure gold,
> And my yield better than choicest silver.
> I walk in the way of righteousness,
> In the midst of the paths of justice,
> To endow those who love me with wealth
> That I may fill their treasuries.

9

PLEASURE

*There was nothing, it seemed, that
grew stale so soon as pleasure.*

F. SCOTT FITZGERALD, *THE BEAUTIFUL AND DAMNED*

Satan cannot create; he can only counterfeit. For example, some people have asserted that pleasure is the devil's phony substitute for happiness. And in fact, this may sometimes be the case. Pleasure can impact our happiness, for better or worse, but it is not the same thing as happiness. It can be defined as that which gratifies, amuses, or satisfies.

On the other hand, we know that pleasure can be good because God engages in it. "For the LORD takes pleasure [*ratsah*] in His people; He will beautify the afflicted ones with salvation" (Psalm 149:4). The Hebrew word *ratsah* means "to be pleased with, to accept favorably."

When Jesus was baptized, the Father expressed His pleasure by saying, "This is My beloved Son, in whom I am well-pleased [*eudokeō*]" (Matthew 3:17). The Greek verb *eudokeō* and related noun *eudokia* simply denote something that is deemed good or pleasing. If God takes pleasure in things, the act cannot be considered wrong.

Furthermore, we can find pleasure in God. "You will make known to me the path of life; in Your presence is fullness of joy; in Your right hand there are pleasures [*na'iym*] forever" (Psalm 16:11). The Hebrew word here is an adjective meaning "delightful, sweet, lovely." (It also means "musical," which suits me well, given my love of music.)

The Hebrew noun *chaphets* and related verb *chephets* are also frequently used to convey something that pleases or displeases God or man. God expressed His displeasure with the rebellious Israelites' sacrifices (Isaiah 1:11). On the Sabbath, man is blessed when forsaking his own pleasure for the Lord (Isaiah 58:13). God says He takes no pleasure in the death of men (Ezekiel 18:32), yet He also expresses His pleasure in carrying out justice upon those who persecute His people (Isaiah 48:14).

In the New Testament, Paul mentions God's pleasure as He fulfilled the work of Christ (Colossians 1:19) and as He works in our lives (Philippians 2:13). Again, there is no inherent quality in this type of pleasure, just the expression of something that is pleasing.

So when does pleasure become a stumbling block or counterfeit substitute for happiness? The New Testament describes a particular pleasure that is negative. The word *hedonism* comes from the Greek *hēdonē*, which denotes a desire for pleasure. It is the idea that pleasure is the most gratifying aspect of life. It's the superficial and artificial satisfaction of an immediate physical or emotional craving—or even a spiritual one. The mantra "If it feels good, do it" sums up this attitude. The resulting emptiness betrays any connection to true happiness. Yet many people go through life mistaking hedonistic pleasure for legitimate joy.

We are warned against this in Jesus' parable of the sower. He describes the "worries and riches and pleasures of this life" as thorns (Luke 8:14). It's an apt comparison because the pursuit of pleasure ensnares people, choking their ability to fulfill their purpose in life. When we routinely seek personal gratification, the ample pleasures of this world crowd out the fruit of the Spirit. We confuse sex with love. We become discontent when not feeling gratified, so we lose our peace. As our pursuit of pleasure becomes more aggressive, we grow impulsive instead of patient, compulsive rather than faithful, self-absorbed instead of kind to others. In all of it, we lose self-control. When pleasure becomes the desire that controls our thoughts and actions, we have given in to hedonism and willingly chosen the wide path of destruction.

The book of Titus describes the hedonistic life as "enslaved to various lusts and pleasures" (Titus 3:3). James describes it as a source of conflict and an obstacle to prayer (James 4:1-3). The derivative *philēdonos* is used to contrast "lovers of pleasure rather than lovers of God" (2 Timothy 3:4). There is also the phrase "wanton pleasure," found in 1 Timothy 5:6 and James 5:5. The Greek word for this phrase, *spatalaō*, means "to live luxuriously." This obsession with luxury and pleasure has been evident throughout history as people have attempted to fill themselves with something other than God. Sadly, it creeps into the church as people confuse materialism with God's blessings. But luxury and earthly pleasures never satisfy. We must drink of the unique joy that Jesus brings to quench our thirst.

It may be helpful to think of most pleasures as junk food. Certain treats, when taken in measured quantity, provide temporary enjoyment without doing any harm. But when eating sweets becomes a way of life and fast food replaces real, nutritious meals, our bodies suffer. Similarly, "he who loves pleasure [*simchah*] will become a poor man; he who loves wine and oil will not become rich" (Proverbs 21:17). Any earthly pleasures—even the good ones—can tempt us toward indulgence if we're not careful. If pleasure becomes our main focus, our heightened desire becomes insatiable and robs us of our real joy.

To avoid the trap of hedonism and wanton pleasure, we must discern the difference between that which is good and that which is bad. Generally, when we take pleasure in good things, our happiness is increased. When we take pleasure in bad things, the false sense of happiness actually works against lasting joy. Taking pleasure in the things that are purely of God will only increase our happiness. For example, we can never get enough of God's presence. Though our cup overflows, there is always more of Him than we will ever be able to experience in this life. The pleasure He brings is always beneficial.

The difficulty for most people is not in the obviously good or bad pleasures, but in those things that throw us off track by subtly rearranging our priorities or distorting our focus. Many men take too much pleasure in their hobbies or work—even the ones we'd rightly call noble or good—by giving them too much importance. Many women derive an unhealthy amount of pleasure from their children or social circles. These are generalities but not atypical.

Personally, I tend to neglect my family or place an undue burden on them so I can participate in ministry. When I am asked to sing or play in the worship band at church, my immediate reaction is *yes!* But because I am aware of this, I purposely set time aside to simply sit in the service with my wife. I also call her and ask her blessing before committing. Given her willingness to please, I have to try to gauge her response from the emotion behind her words. Participating in the worship at church is a wonderful thing, but not at the expense of my marriage or family. Balancing this pleasure in good things with attention to our individual responsibilities and calling requires constant spiritual sensitivity, obedience, and at times, personal sacrifice.

I am probably more sensitive of this ministry trap than most because my father was gone most of my childhood. As he preached to hundreds of thousands of people all over the country in packed coliseums and football stadiums, my mother raised me and my two sisters. Our time with him was feast or famine. When he was in town, he tried to make up for lost time. The intensity was often jarring. When he was gone 300 days out of the year, we got used to it. His time at home demanded that we break our routine to spend time together, and as a child, I was not always prepared to do this. Fortunately, God gave all of us the grace to navigate those challenging times. Some families are not so fortunate. I have seen too many families break apart when children rebelled or couples strayed due to a parent's pursuit of ministry.

Our passion for Christ should always supersede our passion for anything else, but negligence is not a fruit of the Spirit. If a husband is to love his wife as Christ loves the church, and if a father is to lead his children as our heavenly Father guided every step of His Son, we must not abandon our roles as husbands or wives or parents. The pleasure of anything, including ministry, must be balanced with our God-given responsibilities. Even the good things of this world can sour when not held in their proper perspective in the kingdom of God.

Sex

The physical and emotional act of intercourse is perhaps the most misunderstood pleasure in life. Some vilify it as carnal while others regard it as the ultimate gratification. Only by placing it in God's proper perspective can it function as a good, healthy act. When reserved for a man and wife, it becomes an intimate connection. It is impossible for a couple to have a satisfying sex life when harboring negative emotions, such as unforgiveness, anger, or mistrust. The physical closeness should reflect a spiritual unity.

Obviously, adultery works against the marital bond. Unfaithfulness never ends well. Infidelity either destroys a relationship or demands a lengthy and painful reconciliation. The short-term pleasure of sex with one who is not your partner creates massive long-term unhappiness. Yet many people don't consider their own joy, much less that of their spouse, when tempted with the quick fix of physical gratification.

For those who are not married, sex has a less evident barrier, but complications still lurk. The uncertainty of sexually transmitted diseases and unwanted pregnancies should give people pause before engaging in sexual pleasure, but one only has to look around to see how shortsighted people can be. On an emotional and spiritual level, sex without a lifetime commitment creates a web of negative reactions. Disappointment, shame, anger, guilt, regret, loneliness, confusion, and many other damaging consequences are exponentially magnified when sex is involved. Truly, the happiest path is the one laid out in scripture: love, commitment, and then a lifetime of pleasure.

10

FAMILY

*My wife and family received me with great surprise
and joy, because they concluded me certainly dead;
but I must freely confess the sight of them filled
me only with hatred, disgust, and contempt.*

JONATHAN SWIFT, *GULLIVER'S TRAVELS*

Of all the things that can either diminish our happiness or increase it, perhaps the strongest earthly influence comes from our own family. Consider the words of Solomon:

- "A wise son makes a father glad [*samach*], but a foolish son is a grief to his mother" (Proverbs 10:1).

- "He who sires a fool does so to his sorrow, and the father of a fool has no joy [*simchah*]" (Proverbs 17:21).

- "The father of the righteous will greatly rejoice [*giyl*], and he who sires a wise son will be glad [*samach*] in him. Let your father and your mother be glad [*samach*], and let her rejoice [*giyl*] who gave birth to you" (Proverbs 23:24-25).

These passages contrast the results of good and bad behavior in children. Obviously, when our children are righteous, life is wonderful, but when they are foolish or downright evil, we are heartbroken. This goes all the way back to the foundation of mankind—Cain and Abel are the archetypical bad and good sons. We can imagine the pain that Cain caused Adam and Eve by murdering his brother, not to mention their subsequent loss when Cain was banished. The first parents must have felt a double loss caused by sin in their immediate family.

People certainly have the power to bring us happiness. We can give joy to others, and they can bring joy to us. Deuteronomy 24:5 gives a law regarding newlyweds by instructing, "When a man takes a new wife, he shall not go out with the army nor be charged with any duty; he shall be free at home one year and shall give happiness [*samach*] to his wife whom he has taken." With age, this should not diminish, as Solomon wrote: "Let your fountain be blessed, and rejoice [*samach*] in the wife of your youth" (Proverbs 5:18).

God's people are clearly designed to give happiness to others, especially within the family. When God created the world, He populated it first with a man, then his wife, and then their children. He gave them the framework for happiness, but sin disrupted the harmony.

A wayward spouse, child, or parent does not please us. Entrusting an unsaved loved family member to the Lord is a difficult and grievous thing. Yet at the same time, happiness is God's gift to us, so these two opposing forces must be reconciled.

I believe that it's a matter of the greater power. If we are to believe 1 John 4:4, which says, "Greater is He who is in you than he who is in the world," then the stronger force comes from within the believer through the presence of the Holy Spirit. This supernatural happiness has the power to overcome the grief and sorrow brought by family members. In a sense, this is true of all of the things that can potentially rob us of our joy, but it is probably more difficult to deal with in human relationships than in any other situation.

Our families can be sources of joy, but they should never be the source of our greatest joy. That position belongs solely to God. This is why Jesus said, "If anyone comes to Me, and does not hate his own father and mother and wife and children and brothers and sisters, yes, and even his own life, he cannot be My disciple" (Luke 14:26).

This is a comparative statement, not a command to hate everyone, including ourselves. Of Jesus' two great commandments, the first is "love your neighbor as yourself," so there has to be a place for the love of self and others. But when compared to the love we should have for our Savior, it becomes the lesser sentiment.

One of the biggest reasons people lack happiness has to do with family members who inflict pain and cause legitimate sorrow through their sinful words and actions. When my first child was born, I spent the first night at home rocking her while my wife got some well-deserved sleep. In the darkness of my living room, I was overcome with a joy I had never felt. I was a father! Being adopted, I had never known anyone who was "flesh of my flesh." As I held this child of mine, I wept with overwhelming happiness.

A few years after my first son was born, I discovered something else I had never experienced. Our two children were playing one day when, as children do, they got into a fight. My daughter pushed my son off of a swing, and he smacked his head pretty hard. As my wife checked him for serious damage, I dealt with my daughter. I don't think I had ever been so angry. "I love you," I told her, "but I love him too. I will defend both of you with my life, but when you're the one hurting him, you are on the wrong side of my love. *Nothing* makes me angrier than someone hurting a child of mine, so you don't want to be that person!"

I don't know how much she really understood, but at that moment, I understood something profound. When we hurt each other as God's children, we put ourselves on the wrong side of His love and face His wrath. And when we are hurt by others, God races to comfort us. We must allow His comfort to console us and trust Him to deal with those who hurt us—even family members. If we love people more than we love God, we will be robbed of our joy. But if we love the Lord with all of our heart, soul, and mind, then nothing can take away the joy that comes from Jesus Christ.

In the case of family members, this requires a supernatural amount of trust. We cannot control what others do. The prodigal son is not only a picture of each of us in relationship to God but also a depiction of a chronic problem with mankind. Like the father in that story, we must release our loved ones even when doing so causes us sorrow. In that release, which requires us to trust God's sovereignty, there is permission to maintain our happiness. We are not happy that a loved one has strayed, but we do not forfeit the joy of the Lord and the fruit of the Holy Spirit. We should never feel guilty for possessing joy, even when our loved ones suffer the consequences of their sin. God promises to comfort us. By placing our family in their proper place and trusting God through every circumstance, we can maintain a healthy perspective and avoid forfeiting our God-given happiness.

11

WORK

*Work at it, if necessary, early and late, in
season and out of season, not leaving a stone
unturned, and never deferring for a single hour
that which can be done just as well now.*

P.T. BARNUM, *THE ART OF MONEY GETTING*

When Adam and Eve were banished from the Garden of Eden, part of the curse man brought on himself was more difficulty in his work. "Cursed is the ground because of you; in toil you will eat of it all the days of your life. Both thorns and thistles it shall grow for you; and you will eat the plants of the field; by the sweat of your face you will eat bread" (Genesis 3:17-19).

Yet by the book of Psalms, work was not characterized as a curse. And by the New Testament, Jesus was telling parables extolling the virtues of work. So what is the proper perspective on work? It seems fairly obvious to say that work can be both a blessing and a curse. Compared to the bountiful fruit naturally growing in Eden, the uncertainty related to work and survival would be a reduction in blessing, if not a curse. So what differentiates work that is good from that which is bad?

> How blessed [*'esher*] is everyone who fears the LORD,
> Who walks in His ways.
> When you shall eat of the fruit of your hands,
> You will be happy [*'esher*] and it will be well [*towb*] with you
> (Psalm 128:1-2).

Note the precursor to happiness—the reward of eating "the fruit of your hands." The scriptures repeatedly point to the fear of the Lord as the starting point for many blessings: wisdom, knowledge, longevity, riches, honor, security, life, and more. Interestingly, the word translated *blessed* in verse 1 is *'esher*, a noun that is also translated *happiness*. Verse 4 is similar: "Thus shall the man be blessed who fears the LORD," but this time, the word translated *blessed* is *barak*, a verb sometimes translated *kneel*. When we reverently and respectfully submit to the Lord and walk in His ways, we will find happiness in our work. We will *towb*—be joyful, glad, and pleased.

Godly work includes two things: seeking Him first and working diligently.

I worked at a Fortune 500 company for a while. The salary and the benefits were the best I had ever had, so that was a blessing when I sorely needed it. But after a short time, I noticed that many of the people climbing the corporate ladder frequently mistreated others and neglected their families to move up the pay scale. I quickly concluded that I would focus on obeying the Lord more than any other factor regardless of whether I drew a salary from a large corporation, worked freelance, or devoted all my time to ministry efforts. For me, that meant leaving the comfort and stability of the big company to venture into an internet start-up that provided content filtering.

We were one of the early groups in that space at a time when people were still discovering the vast amount of online pornography and child predation. Much of my time went into helping parents and law enforcement officials police the internet and protect children. That was much more fulfilling than my previous work. Eventually, I left there to return to full-time ministry. Everyone's calling is unique and may go through different seasons, as mine has, but the core issue is the same: obedience to God's will.

I should note that many people differentiate between career and ministry. Granted, we use the phrase *working in the ministry* to refer to full-time employment at a church or parachurch organization. But real ministry does not depend on the tax classification of your business. We can be in ministry regardless of our employment. I met a man who left the business world to work for a Bible distribution organization, only to be disillusioned by the amount of ordinary business he had to perform. On the other hand, I have known many businessmen and women who have ministered to their coworkers on a level that a church or Christian nonprofit organization never could. Ministry is a state of mind, not a creation of the state.

When our chief pursuit is the Lord and His kingdom work, we will find happiness regardless of the position or pay. We must never fall for the false notion of job security. Christ is our real security in every employment situation. The important thing is that we seek His will and that we work.

Diligent work requires honesty, effort, and wisdom. The mentality of entitlement and welfare is not scriptural.

> If anyone is not willing to work, then he is not to eat, either. For we hear that some among you are leading an undisciplined life, doing no work at all, but acting like busybodies. Now such persons we command and exhort in the Lord Jesus Christ to work in quiet fashion and eat their own bread (2 Thessalonians 3:10-12).

Imagine the change in work ethic that would take place if those who refused to work were given no food! I dare say our welfare budgets would shrink dramatically. Note that Paul does not say that those who are unable to work should not eat. Caring for the disabled and the sick is entirely scriptural. The Bible also commands us to give food to the poor. But it never allows for laziness. We should "eat our own bread" by working to the best of our ability.

The writer of Ecclesiastes said, "The sleep of the working man is pleasant, whether he eats little or much; but the full stomach of the rich man does not allow him to sleep" (Ecclesiastes 5:12). In this context, the word *rich* refers to those who love money and stingily hoard it. Those who work honestly for a living will be satisfied regardless of their financial status, but without a godly attitude, even those who have great wealth will lack peace.

Jesus' parable about the talents (units of money) illustrates several points related to work. In this story, a wealthy man gives his servants different amounts of money, each "according to his own ability," and then goes on a journey. When he returns, he finds that two of the servants—one given five talents and the other given two talents—each doubled their money. The third servant was given one talent. He hadn't lost any money, but he hadn't gained any either. The master promotes the first two and punishes the third, calling him wicked and lazy.

There are several lessons to be drawn here, but I want to stress three that are related to work. First, we are not all equal in our ability. Some people know how to make money. For others, it's a more arduous task. Second, equality in income is a false expectation. Spirituality should never be measured in financial terms. God does not give the same amount of money to everyone, so man's attempts to equalize income cannot be considered godly or compassionate. Third, we are expected to do something with what we are given, whether large or small. Doing nothing is considered wicked and lazy.

Andy Andrews, a motivational storyteller and gifted author, talks about this. "God feeds the birds, but He doesn't throw the worms in their nests! For those of us who have the ability to do something, it is incumbent upon us to do just that…something. Even when we don't know what to do, we must do something." He should know. Andy once lived under a pier on the beach, homeless and destitute. But by submitting His life to the Lord and practicing a godly work ethic, he not only survived, he thrived. He now teaches others to make themselves valuable. Simply finding a need and filling it is a proven formula for success.

Labor can be difficult, but productivity is always rewarding. Therefore, we must always work with diligence and zeal. "Whatever you do," Paul wrote, "do your work heartily, as for the Lord rather than for men, knowing that from the Lord you will receive the reward of the inheritance. It is the Lord Christ whom you serve" (Colossians 3:23-24).

When we pursue the Lord through our work, whatever it may be, we will find that work is not a curse, but a blessing. We will sleep well, be content, and walk in the favor of the Lord.

Provision

As we obediently work, we must never forget the true source of the blessings we reap.

> You visit the earth and cause it to overflow;
> You greatly enrich it;
> The stream of God is full of water;
> You prepare their grain, for thus You prepare the earth.
> You water its furrows abundantly,
> You settle its ridges,
> You soften it with showers,
> You bless its growth (Psalm 65:9-10).

The American idea of self-sufficiency properly places the burden on each of us to perform to the best of our ability, yet it is somewhat misleading. No millionaire is ever self-made. Any wealth we accrue is merely borrowed for a short span of time. If we think we provide for ourselves, we are self-deluded. One natural disaster, war, financial meltdown, or other calamity can strip us of everything. Ultimately, death takes every penny we have ever earned. We start broke, and we end broke. In between, we rely on God's earth to function as He designed, where our work results in provision.

To use the farming analogy, we are expected to sow seeds into fertile soil and reap the harvest when it comes due. But we must never forget that God must send the rain and sun in order for anything to grow. We must do our part, but God is our provider.

Fear

I love it when the great philosophers get things only half right. Seneca, the revered Spanish-Roman writer who lived during Jesus' time, saw only half the picture in his musings on the subject of happiness. Fear is typically depicted as negative, even in much Christian thought. It is not. The determining factor lies in the object of our fear.

When Joseph was testing his brothers, he said to them, "Do this and live, for I fear God" (Genesis 42:18). This was his oath, his guarantee that his word was true—he feared.

When the Egyptian king commanded the Hebrew midwives to kill the Hebrews' newborn males, they ignored his edict because they feared God (Exodus 1:17,21). They did not do evil because they feared.

After the Israelites fled Egyptian slavery and spent 40 years in the wilderness, God parted the waters of the Jordan River so they could enter the promised land. But Joshua explained that the miracle had a deeper significance. "The LORD your God dried up the waters…that all the peoples of the earth may know that the hand of the LORD is mighty, so that you may fear the LORD your God forever" (Joshua 4:23-24). God miraculously delivered His people so they would fear.

The Holy Spirit told King David, "He who rules over men righteously, who rules in the fear of God, is as the light of the morning when the sun rises" (2 Samuel 23:3-4). A righteous leader fears.

Consider this incomplete list of what happens when we fear God.

- He delivers us (2 Kings 17:39).

- He reveals Himself to us (Psalm 25:14).

- He stores up His goodness for us (Psalm 31:19).

- He watches over us (Psalm 33:18).

- He sends His angels and rescues us (Psalm 34:7).

- He blesses us (Psalm 67:7).

- Salvation comes to us (Psalm 85:9).

- He has compassion on us (Psalm 103:13).

- We gain wisdom (Psalm 111:10).

- Our life is prolonged (Proverbs 10:27).

- We gain confidence (Proverbs 14:26).

- We are rescued from evil (Proverbs 16:6).

- We are healed (Malachi 4:2).

- We are motivated to witness (2 Corinthians 5:11).

- We become holy (2 Corinthians 7:1).

Suddenly, fear does not sound like such a negative experience! But here's the key: Only God should be the object of our fear. Fearing the pure and mighty Creator of the universe is not only natural but also proper. Why is this fear different? Because "the fear of the LORD is clean, enduring forever" (Psalm 19:9).

Jesus clearly divided good fear from the bad when He said, "Do not fear those who kill the body but are unable to kill the soul; but rather fear Him who is able to destroy both soul and body in hell" (Matthew 10:28).

However, fear is merely the starting place; it is not the endgame. Ironically, fearing God is the first step to overcoming every other fear. When we fear the Lord, we do not fear anything else, including...

- other gods (2 Kings 17:38)
- the future (1 Chronicles 28:20)
- evil or evil men (Psalm 23:4; 2 Chronicles 32:7)
- the armies of the enemy (2 Kings 6:16)
- natural disasters (Psalm 46:2)
- persecution (John 20:19)
- suffering (Revelation 2:10)
- death (Matthew 10:28)

When we are on the right side of fear, it's not a hindrance to happiness—it's a pathway to it. When we fear God, He can comfort us.

When God called His people to repentance, warning them of the destruction their rebellion would bring if they did not turn back to Him, He said, "Do not fear, O land, rejoice [*giyl*] and be glad [*samach*], for the Lord has done great things" (Joel 2:21). As the Israelites were rebuilding the temple, God spoke through His prophet saying, "As for the promise which I made you when you came out of Egypt, My Spirit is abiding in your midst; do not fear!" (Haggai 2:5).

When an angel appeared to Zacharias, "fear gripped him." But the angel told him, "Do not be afraid" (Luke 1:12-13). When the disciples were afraid, Jesus comforted them: "Peace I leave with you; My peace I give to you; not as the world gives do I give to you. Do not let your heart be troubled, nor let it be fearful" (John 14:27). And in an interesting juxtaposition of these two emotions, when the two women discovered Jesus' resurrection, "they left the tomb quickly with fear and great joy [*chara*]" (Matthew 28:8).

John wrote that "perfect love casts out fear" (1 John 4:18). The only perfect love is Jesus Christ. Fearing God compels us to seek His presence, which drives out every destructive fear.

Psychiatrists have diagnosed a wide range of fears. Researching all of the phobias is revealing and, at times, humorous. From ablutophobia (fear of washing or bathing) to zemmiphobia (fear of the great mole rat), men have categorized and sought treatment for everything imaginable. People fear heights and widths, open spaces and enclosed rooms, water and dryness, wealth and poverty, day and night. We live in a phobiaphobic world. Doctors tend to medicate, but the Divine Healer wants to eradicate. We were created to fear only God, who seeks to give us comfort and peace in the midst of every storm. Once we understand and implement this truth, our minds are free from trouble, and we experience a supernatural joy more powerful than anything in this world.

Promises of God

I have flown on various airplanes all around the world—a single-engine prop plane around Texas, a seaplane in Alaska, a semiretired World War II plane in Romania, a small jet across southern Africa...you name it, I've ridden in it. After our first two children were born, I developed a serious fear of flying. It stemmed less from the act of flying than it did the fear of dying and leaving my wife and small children to fend for themselves. For some reason, the fear manifested itself with airplanes. Statistically, flying is safer than driving, yet I've never had any problem driving. I've driven from Oregon to New Hampshire in less than three days. I've navigated switchbacks in a Rocky Mountain snowstorm in the middle of the night. I face rush-hour traffic almost daily. I have even driven into Lower Manhattan!

It's not completely logical, but I am always white-knuckled during takeoff. Perhaps it's the lack of control a passenger has in the air. Or perhaps it's the process of putting a huge amount of weight in a metal tube with proportionally tiny wings and hurling it into the air with burning, explosive fuel at high speeds. Whatever the case, I began to experience the kind of fear that keeps you up at night worrying about a next-day departure. Turbulence has been known to cause me to pray out loud.

Against this backdrop of worsening fear, I was set to travel to Rwanda, via Europe, on a mission trip. I never wanted to give in to the fear because I knew it was not of God, but needless to say, I was uptight. I made it through takeoff and the first few hours, but then, somewhere over the cold, deep Atlantic, we flew into a storm. As we rocked and jolted, I was a wreck.

I must have been just like the disciples on that storm-stricken boat as

Jesus slept. I begged God to do something. Stop the turbulence. Give me peace. Just tell me that I would make it to Africa and back safely. Anything.

I am not the type to claim I hear God often outside of His word in scripture. It's not that I don't believe He talks to us, it's just that I distrust my own mind and imagination. I am hesitant to attribute my thoughts, even if inspired by truth, to His voice. But in this case, I fully believe I heard God.

As I prayed—or more accurately, panicked—five words came out of nowhere: "You will see your grandchildren." That was it. One short sentence filled with more assurance than I realized at the time. I am convinced it was God for several reasons: First, it was not specifically what I wanted to hear. I was hoping for "You'll be fine." Or maybe "Be still, O thou mighty storm." You know, something that sounds like God is supposed to sound. What I got was bigger than one trip to Africa. It was beyond the scope of my shortsightedness—far beyond. The fear subsided. I still don't like flying, but I don't live in fear. I battle it, but every time it crops up, I say, "I will see my grandchildren" and go about my business.

What's more amazing about that promise is what happened a dozen years later. When my retina detached, first in one eye and then in the other, I heard all the potential problems (many of which I still have) and read the statistics on blindness. Modern science is wonderful, but I still face the prospect of unexpected and sudden blindness in one or both eyes.

But I have a promise from God—a phrase I would not have come up with on my own. "*You will* see *your grandchildren!*"

Now that's a promise. I was worried about one trip on an airplane, and God generously gave me words to carry me far beyond a single journey to Africa. Through all of my optical difficulty, I have had no fear. None. I have God's promise, so it's as good as done. I will see my grandchildren.

A promise is a declaration of what someone will or will not do. It gives an expectation of fulfillment. I find it interesting that the Hebrew word frequently used to this action is *dabar*, which means both "to speak" and "to promise." When God speaks a word, it is better than any human promise because the very act of Him speaking it makes it true.

The best cure for fear is a word from God. We must choose to believe it, but when we put our trust in Him, we can stand on it with absolute assurance. Fortunately, you don't have to be on an airplane over the Atlantic

Ocean to receive His promises. The Bible is loaded with them. Anything He says is a promise upon which you can depend.

God spoke a promise to His people through the prophet Isaiah: "Do not fear, for I am with you; do not anxiously look about you, for I am your God. I will strengthen you, surely I will help you, surely I will uphold you with My righteous right hand" (Isaiah 41:10).

Throughout the ancient covenant, God promised a Messiah: "But as for you, Bethlehem...from you One will go forth for Me to be ruler in Israel" (Micah 5:2).

The Old Testament ends with a promise: "He [the prophet] will restore the hearts of the fathers to their children and the hearts of the children to their fathers, so that I [God] will not come and smite the land with a curse" (Malachi 4:6).

The birth of Jesus Christ was announced with a promise to Mary:

> The angel said to her, "Do not be afraid, Mary; for you have found favor [*charis*] with God. And behold, you will conceive in your womb and bear a son, and you shall name Him Jesus. He will be great and will be called the Son of the Most High; and the Lord God will give Him the throne of His father David; and He will reign over the house of Jacob forever, and His kingdom will have no end" (Luke 1:30-33).

Jesus left the earth with a promise: "I am with you always, even to the end of the age" (Matthew 28:20).

Paul wrote about the dependability of God's promises to the church in Corinth when he said, "For as many as are the promises of God, in Him [Jesus Christ] they are yes" (2 Corinthians 1:20).

The Bible ends with the promise of Jesus' return: "Yes, I am coming quickly" (Revelation 22:20).

The entire Bible is God's promise to redeem mankind. Every fear that threatens to steal our faith, joy, peace, and confidence can be rebutted with a promise in scripture. When we take God at His word, which is rock-solid and dependable, we have no reason to fear anything in this world. That's a promise you can take to the grave—and beyond.

Caution

A smart warrior does not embrace fear, but demonstrates caution. In Judges 7, when Gideon was winnowing his army down from 10,000 men, he took them to a stream to drink. Those who knelt down, putting themselves in a vulnerable position, were sent home. Those who cupped their hands and lapped the water from them, keeping their heads up and eyes open, were kept.

Peter encouraged this quality in the early believers. "Be of sober spirit, be on the alert. Your adversary, the devil, prowls around like a roaring lion, seeking someone to devour" (1 Peter 5:8). We are not controlled by fear, but we should be aware that we live in a hostile world. We must be vigilant and on guard both in the natural and supernatural. We have confidence when we are on God's side, but the ongoing battle between good and evil requires us to be cautious.

13

BROKENNESS

He was beaten (he knew that); but he was not broken.

JACK LONDON, *THE CALL OF THE WILD*

Life can break us. Divorce, abuse, loss, failure, disappointment, and dozens of other circumstances can leave us empty, disheartened, and unhappy. Like a dog that has been beaten, we go through life with our heads down and our tails between our legs. Brokenness is not so much a negative emotion, like anger or envy, but a lack of emotion. It's an indifference to our own lives and numbness toward those around us.

In his despair, Job cried out, "My spirit is broken [*chabal*], my days are extinguished, the grave is ready for me" (Job 17:1). The Hebrew word here is not an adjective, as it reads in English. It is a verb. It means "to be ruined, corrupted, destroyed." This type of brokenness is not merely a feeling; it is something that occurs. It's an erosion of purpose and meaning. When you're broken in this way, you believe your life is ruined. Like Job, you feel as if you could die and it wouldn't matter. "Who can see any hope for me?" he asked (verse 15 NIV).

If you believe *chabal* is your lot in life, you need a Job experience. God

Almighty came into his ruined life and challenged his mind-set, saying something like this: "What do you know? You're a man, and I am God. Don't you think I can do better than this for you?"

Job agreed. He repented and turned from his grief, self-pity, and despair. "I know that You can do all things," he confessed, "and that no purpose of Yours can be thwarted" (Job 42:2). Job was one of the most tormented men in history, but God gave him a good life. "The LORD blessed the latter days of Job more than his beginning" (verse 12).

If you have reached this point of brokenness, the remedy is to repent of your despair and trust God to restore you. The beginning may have been bad, but that doesn't mean the latter days can't be fulfilling and happy.

This is God's desire for all of us. It was His desire for the Israelites, who were repeatedly broken and enslaved, when He declared, "For I know the plans that I have for you…plans for welfare and not for calamity to give you a future and a hope" (Jeremiah 29:11). It should be noted that the word translated here as *welfare* has a different connotation from the way we use it today. It doesn't refer to government-run handouts. The Hebrew word means "completeness, soundness, peace." It is the opposite of brokenness at the hands of the enemy.

However, there is a type of brokenness that comes from God. It is found in the passage where King David repents after his affair with Bathsheba. "Make me to hear joy [*sasown*] and gladness [*simchah*], let the bones which You have broken [*dakah*] rejoice [*giyl*]" (Psalm 51:8).

As you can see, this passage is also loaded with happiness! There is a contrast between a broken life and a happy life, but there is also a significant difference between David's brokenness and Job's. Job felt overwhelmed by ruin and corruption (*chabal*), but the word *dakah* means "to be crushed, contrite." Most importantly, though, is the phrase "which You have broken." Job's brokenness came from the calamity and despondency that had fallen upon him. David's brokenness came from godly conviction and repentance. Job's brokenness threatened to destroy him. David's promised to restore him. In this scenario, God uses brokenness to bring happiness.

Later in that same passage, David writes, "The sacrifices of God are a broken [*shabar*] spirit; a broken and a contrite [*dakah*] heart, O God, You will not despise" (verse 17).

This third verb, *shabar*, means "to wreck, maim, violently rend, or break in pieces." It is the Hebrew word most commonly translated "broken" in the Old Testament. The New Testament Greek equivalent is *syntribō*, as in the crucifixion passage, "Not a bone of Him shall be broken" (John 19:36; see Psalm 34:20).

This type of brokenness broadly covers the anguish of saints and the punishment of sinners. On one side, God promises through His prophet, "I will seek the lost, bring back the scattered, bind up the broken [*shabar*] and strengthen the sick" (Ezekiel 34:16). On the other, we are warned, "A man who hardens his neck after much reproof will suddenly be broken [*shabar*] beyond remedy" (Proverbs 29:1).

Once again, we see this pattern of human destruction and divine restoration. Only our own attitudes can cause self-inflicted brokenness or prevent God's healing intervention. This is a crucial point related to happiness because the notion that we should live in brokenness is not according to God's plan as long as we are surrendered to Him. There is no brokenness that God cannot and will not heal when we yield to His will and admit that His words are true. If we stand in opposition to God and His word, however, we will not be restored—we will be broken.

So the question for each of us is this: Will we take a contrite heart to God and let Him turn our brokenness into joy, or will we choose our own pride and suffer the brokenness that destroys?

You can almost tell people's answer to this question simply by looking at them. In addition to the three Hebrew verbs, the Old Testament includes an adjective for *broken* (*nake'*), which appears in such passages as these:

- "A joyful [*sameach*] heart makes a cheerful [*yatab*] face, but when the heart is sad, the spirit is broken [*nake'*]" (Proverbs 15:13).

- "A joyful [*sameach*] heart is good medicine, but a broken [*nake'*] spirit dries up the bones" (Proverbs 17:22).

The other translation for this adjective is *stricken*, and that aptly fits those whose joy has departed. Unhappiness is a disease we wear on our face. But when we allow God to intervene, our countenance changes. Brokenness in any form, whether from ruinous circumstances, wrecked pride, or a contrite heart, visibly robs us of our joy. Only God can restore us, and that is precisely what He wants to do.

If your brokenness comes from a contrite, repentant heart, that's great news. You are about to experience more joy than you previously had. If your brokenness feels like hopeless ruin, you are not in agreement with God. Apply the remedy—repentance and realignment with His word—and your latter days will be better than the former, and your countenance will reflect God's gracious restoration.

Grief

Losing a loved one is naturally a sorrowful experience. Grief is not condemned in the Bible. When Lazarus died, Jesus wept even though He knew He was about to raise him from the dead! God understands our pain. Yet in the Sermon on the Mount, Jesus promised to console us in our grief. "Blessed are those who mourn, for they shall be comforted" (Matthew 5:4). Paul explained that believers should not "grieve as do the rest who have no hope" (1 Thessalonians 4:13).

When we know that a deceased loved one experienced salvation, the hope we have in Christ should carry us through the temporary loss. The more difficult loss is that of those whose salvation is unknown. This requires a deep trust in the sovereignty of God and a daily reliance on the comfort of the Holy Spirit.

14

Suffering

> *Suffering has been stronger than all other*
> *teaching, and has taught me to understand*
> *what your heart used to be. I have been bent and*
> *broken, but—I hope—into a better shape.*
>
> Charles Dickens, *Great Expectations*

On December 4, 2009, Matt Chandler was diagnosed with a malignant, cancerous brain tumor. At the time, Matt was the pastor of the Village Church in Dallas, a husband, and the father of three young children. In a matter of days, he went from living the life of a dynamic, up-and-coming preacher to having a craniotomy to remove a portion of his brain and beginning a fierce regimen of radiation and chemotherapy. A few months later, I met him when he was on *LIFE Today*. He is one of the most amazing people I have ever met.

Circumstances like Matt's can test one's faith, but he was profoundly strengthened and deepened. From an outside perspective, his suffering is puzzling. Here's a young guy fulfilling the Great Commission, raising a beautiful family, and generally living a righteous life. If anyone didn't deserve to go through so much pain, Matt Chandler and his family certainly didn't.

His story brings to life the occasion recorded in the Gospel of John:

> As he went along, he saw a man blind from birth. His disciples asked him, "Rabbi, who sinned, this man or his parents, that he was born blind?"
>
> "Neither this man nor his parents sinned," said Jesus, "but this happened so that the works of God might be displayed in him" (John 9:1-3 NIV).

The first part of the disciples' question is almost nonsensical. If the man was born blind, how could he have been struck blind because of his own sin? The question of his parents' sin harkens back to the generational blessings and curses of the Old Testament, but Jesus rejects that notion too. Instead, He says something that's even more perplexing to the human mind—the man had suffered his entire life in order to show the world the works of God! Of course, in that man's case, this meaning became immediately clear as Jesus healed him. Naturally, the miracle blew everyone's minds, and people instantly believed that Jesus was the Christ. But what if, as with countless people since Jesus' time, the man had not been healed? Could the same be said of his suffering? Even Jesus didn't heal every sick person He passed. Can the works of God be displayed in the life of someone who is not healed?

Matt Chandler's testimony addresses this difficult question. When I met Matt, he explained his faith by relating the story of Shadrach, Meshach, and Abednego as they faced death in the fiery furnace. This is what they said to King Nebuchadnezzar, whom they had offended by not bowing down to his idols:

> If we are thrown into the blazing furnace, the God we serve is able to deliver us from it, and he will deliver us from Your Majesty's hand. But even if he does not, we want you to know, Your Majesty, that we will not serve your gods or worship the image of gold you have set up (Daniel 3:17-18 NIV).

"That's where I'm standing," Matt Chandler said. "God can heal me. I believe He will heal me. I believe I'm going to be an old, surly Baptist preacher. But even if He doesn't…" Matt went on to cite Paul's words in Philippians 1:21. "For to me, to live is Christ and to die is gain."

At the time of this writing, Matt is still battling and suffering. By the time you read this, Matt may be healed, or he may be gone from this earth. But whatever the outcome, I can tell you firsthand that God can be glorified through mankind's suffering.

On the one-year anniversary of his craniotomy, Matt wrote this in his blog:

> I am primarily known as a pastor and preacher, but here's the truth that slammed into me when I was wrestling with God over this surgery. One day I am not going to preach or pastor; one day I am not going to be Lauren's husband or my kids' father. All the things that define me here will be gone, and I will simply be His. I'm still meditating on that. That's all I really am…*His.*

So here's the question related to the topic of this book. Can we be happy in that simple reality—we are His—even in our suffering? Sadly, most of us are not, despite the fact that we will probably never experience the level of uncertainty and pain Matt has endured. Yet this is the only purpose of suffering defined by Christ Himself—to glorify God.

Jesus was not indifferent to suffering. He knew it well. In fact, He chose it for our sake. And it's hard to imagine that He did not possess joy, even in the anguish. He even told us to be happy if we are made to suffer for His sake.

> Blessed are you when people insult you and persecute you, and falsely say all kinds of evil against you because of Me. Rejoice [*chairō*] and be glad [*agalliaō*], for your reward in heaven is great; for in the same way they persecuted the prophets who were before you (Matthew 5:11-12).

Nothing will test your joy like suffering. It would be disingenuous to argue that it's not hard. It's very difficult. The imagery of a fiery furnace in the book of Daniel is appropriate because pain can consume us in an instant. But even though pain and suffering can rob us of our comfort, our abilities, and even our lives, it does not have to steal our joy. Why? Because of God's promise that the suffering will end.

"Precious in the sight of the LORD is the death of His godly ones" (Psalm 116:15). We view death as the end, but God views it as a transition from one place to another. And to Him, it is a wonderful thing. But what of the suffering that often precedes death? Or even the suffering that does not kill but instead makes life unbearable?

The phrase "the joy of the Lord is your strength" comes from the story of Nehemiah, who was the governor at a time when the Israelites had suffered as slaves under the Babylonians for 70 years. In Nehemiah 9:37, God's people made this lament: "The kings…rule over our bodies and over our cattle as they please, so we are in great distress."

One day, Ezra, the priest and scribe, brought out the Book of the Law of Moses and read it out loud from daybreak until noon so that the people could hear God's promises to deliver them through their suffering. They listened to the word of God, wept as it was read, and then worshipped together. Then Nehemiah made this proclamation: "Go, eat of the fat, drink of the sweet, and send portions to him who has nothing prepared; for this day is holy to our Lord. Do not be grieved, for the joy [*chedvah*] of the LORD is your strength" (Nehemiah 8:10).

There, in the midst of their suffering and weeping, is happiness—the kind that comes from God and penetrates all circumstances. This Hebrew word *chedvah* is the same one used when the ark of the covenant was brought into David's tent and the people presented a psalm of thanksgiving for the Lord's presence, saying, "Splendor and majesty are before Him, strength and joy [*chedvah*] are in His place" (1 Chronicles 16:27).

Joy is what comforts us through grief and suffering. It may feel muted, but it need not be lost. We don't give in to the suffering, but rather give in to God *through* the suffering. My pastor, Bill Ramsey Jr., says, "God didn't come into the world to get you out of trouble, but to get in the trouble with you." All of us will suffer to some degree. Some will suffer in ways we do not understand. But God promises to be with us in the midst of it, and in that, there is joy.

PART 3

PATHS TO HAPPINESS

Some principles are true in every situation. Water will always flow downhill because the law of gravity is not conditional. Similarly, every time we engage in certain activities and adopt particular attitudes, we move in the right direction. These are guaranteed paths to an increased level of happiness.

15

SALVATION

Do not complain, for it is for you that I came,
and my journey will be your salvation.

ALEXANDRÉ DUMAS, *THE COUNT OF MONTE CRISTO*

This is where it all begins. If you have not experienced salvation through Jesus Christ, I have very little for you. If you do not enter into life's journey with the promised Messiah as your guide, you face the possibility of a painful, meaningless life. You may go partway down the path of happiness by engaging in the things that are eternally true, such as helping others or gaining wisdom or getting rid of bitterness and fear, but you will eventually come to an impasse. The chasm of sin is too wide to cross alone.

Perhaps you can find some happiness in the pleasures of money, food, drink, sex, power, fame, or any of the other things the world has to offer, but they too will eventually fail. One only has to look at the long list of celebrity suicides and drug overdoses to know that such things don't guarantee happiness and, in many instances, only make life more miserable. From Ernest Hemingway and Kurt Cobain (suicides) to Judy Garland and Chris Farley (overdoses), an alarmingly large number of people seemed to have it all but ended with nothing. If all you have is this life… well, good luck. There's too much emptiness and pain for me to see any path to long-lasting happiness.

If you have not excluded the possibility of a Savior but have not yet partaken of His grace, there is still hope. In fact, it's probably just what you're looking for. Salvation is the point where it all originates—where all things are made new, where the old things pass away and new life begins. Salvation is the second chance we all need. It is the eternal perspective that carries us through this temporary life.

> How long must I wrestle with my thoughts
> and day after day have sorrow in my heart?
> How long will my enemy triumph over me?…
> But I trust in your unfailing love;
> my heart rejoices [*giyl*] in your salvation.
> I will sing the Lord's praise,
> for he has been good to me (Psalm 13:2,5-6 niv).

This salvation comes only through Jesus Christ. It does not come through our own works. It is not a matter of mind over matter, but God's power over sin. There is no work that you and I can perform to get to heaven on our own. After the fall of mankind, only Jesus Christ could provide a way for sinful people to be reconciled with a perfect Father.

The Messiah's coming was predicted by the prophets of old. "And it will be said in that day, 'Behold, this is our God for whom we have waited that He might save us; this is the Lord for whom we have waited; let us rejoice [*giyl*] and be glad [*samach*] in His salvation'" (Isaiah 25:9).

For a time, sorrow still exists on earth. Jesus did not come to take us away from the things that make us unhappy, but to take us *through* them. That salvation allows us to find a deeper joy during the journey. That's why His arrival was announced with an overwhelmingly happy proclamation: "The angel said to them, 'Do not be afraid; for behold, I bring you good news of great joy [*chara*] which will be for all the people; for today in the city of David there has been born for you a Savior, who is Christ the Lord'" (Luke 2:10-11).

This is the same Messiah whose birth led to Herod's orders to kill all the boys in and around Bethlehem who were two years old and younger.

The same Messiah who was brutally beaten and wrongfully executed. The same Messiah whose disciples were chased, imprisoned, tortured, and killed. So how could the angels promise blessings of joy that would cause us to be happy?

The angels could promise true joy, not because the suffering of this life would disappear, but because the blessing of eternal life had appeared. Happiness ceases to be a temporary condition when we fully understand the gift of salvation. It becomes a permanent part of our character because God has given it and nothing on earth can take it away. The light of this eternal life cannot be snuffed out by the darkness of our temporary sorrows. The purpose of Jesus Christ becomes our purpose. And in that, there is great joy. "These things I have spoken to you," Jesus said, "so that My joy [*chara*] may be in you, and that your joy [*chara*] may be made full" (John 15:11).

If we allow the work of salvation to fully take hold in our lives, happiness will be an inseparable part of it. The message is not misery now, joy later. Jesus said the kingdom of heaven is at hand. It is here now. It began with His birth and continues today if we will let it. Trouble is temporary, but salvation is eternal. We see this principle in the book of Psalms:

> His anger is but for a moment,
> His favor is for a lifetime;
> Weeping may last for the night,
> But a shout of joy [*rinnah*] comes in the morning...
> You have turned for me my mourning into dancing;
> You have loosed my sackcloth and girded me with gladness
> [*simchah*] (Psalm 30:5,11).

The passage does not say there will be no pain—there will be. It simply moves us beyond the affliction to a place of happiness. Morning occurs every day. You cannot stop it. When the salvation of Jesus Christ reigns in our hearts and minds, we cannot hold back the happiness.

I cannot conceive that the original 12 disciples, except for Judas Iscariot, were unhappy people. Following Jesus Christ's crucifixion and resurrection, they went out and preached the gospel. None went on to rule in a palace or become revered members of affluent societies. They were persecuted, and several were murdered by crucifixion or beheading. But overall, were they unhappy?

Before Jesus departed, He appeared to them and breathed on them, saying, "Receive the Holy Spirit" (John 20:21-22). After that, they went out to fulfill the Great Commission. Given the incredible salvation that all of them possessed and the great witness they expressed, they must have exhibited the fruit of the Holy Spirit.

Regardless of what we face in this life, believers own something far more powerful. The result of the blessing of salvation is the promise that we can possess love, peace, patience, kindness, goodness, faithfulness, gentleness, self-control, and joy.

16

GOD'S PRESENCE

*I throw myself down in my chamber, and I call
in and invite God and his angels thither, and
when they are there, I neglect God and his
angels, for the noise of a fly, for the rattling
of a coach, for the whining of a door.*

JOHN DONNE, *AT THE FUNERAL OF SIR WILLIAM COKAYNE*

There is true happiness in the presence of God. In fact, any sense of happiness attributed to anything but God is counterfeit and, in the end, empty. So the question becomes, how do we eliminate the distractions that so easily entice us so we can enter into His presence?

"You will make known to me the path of life; in Your presence is fullness of joy [*simchah*]; in Your right hand there are pleasures forever" (Psalm 16:11). If we want "fullness of joy," then God's presence is essential. His presence is the goal; happiness is the beneficial by-product.

Part of the beauty of the work of Jesus Christ lies in the tearing of the temple veil. When Matthew recorded the death of Jesus, the very next thing he wrote was, "And behold, the veil of the temple was torn in two from top to bottom" (Matthew 27:51). This veil separated the holy place, where the priests ministered, from the holy of holies, where God's Spirit resided. When Christ died, He removed that wall between God and man, making it possible for us to live in His presence. Even today, we still have a tendency to elevate certain people to priestly status, but living in God's presence is not reserved for a few super-spiritual men. It is intended for every believer.

"For You make him most blessed [*bērakah*] forever; You make him joyful [*chadah*] with gladness [*simchah*] in Your presence" (Psalm 21:6). This is God's desire for His children. He longs for intimacy with each of us, and that comes only by spending time together. In scripture, there are four overarching ways to enter into the presence of God.

His Word

The Bible is the simplest place to know God. By reading it, studying it, and meditating on it, we begin to understand the nature and character of God. "For the word of God is living and active" (Hebrews 4:12). There is a level of happiness derived from knowing scripture. All the things that God's word provides, such as wisdom, peace, knowledge, and direction, are natural agents of happiness. Delving into the scriptures for insight allows us to understand who He is personally.

Repeatedly, David talks about the significance of God's word in his life. In Psalm 119, the great poetic dissertation on the word of God, he says, "Your word I have treasured in my heart" (verse 11), and "I have promised to keep Your words" (verse 57), and "I will never forget Your precepts, for by them You have revived me" (verse 93). After such declarations, he says, "Make Your face shine upon Your servant, and teach me Your statutes" (verse 135). This is a clear reference to God's presence. In fact, the Hebrew word translated *face* is *paniym*, which is translated elsewhere as *presence*. When we commit ourselves to His word, we will experience His presence.

Prayer

My wife has an amazing ability to start a conversation, leave the room, and continue it. I completely lack this capability. If she leaves the room, I think we're done. If she does say anything else, I am likely to tune her out, not understand her, or not hear her at all. For the most part, conversation, to me, requires someone's presence. (Phone calls, text messages, e-mails, and other technological advances are the exceptions, but they still require the attention and active engagement of both parties to communicate.)

Given the simple definition of prayer as a conversation, the necessity of God's presence is a given. Of course, we can be like the Pharisee whom Jesus described as praying to himself (Luke 18:11), but true prayer is not to ourselves; it's to God. And that means He hears because He is near. By engaging in two-way communication with God—talking to Him, listening, and reading His written word—we begin to fellowship in the spirit with our Creator and Redeemer.

"God is faithful, through whom you were called into fellowship with His Son, Jesus Christ our Lord" (1 Corinthians 1:9). If we are called into *fellowship* (an intimate word conveying an intense closeness), we must talk to each other in the same room. Prayer should be a two-way dialogue in which God's presence allows us to know Him better—and also find happiness.

Fellowship with Believers

Jesus made perhaps the most straightforward promise of His presence when He said, "For where two or three have gathered together in My name, I am there in their midst" (Matthew 18:20). The most common setting for this in our culture is at church, but that does not exclude His presence in any other setting. You can invite the Lord's presence at work, school, or any other place where people can gather. The key here is the phrase *in My name*.

Under the old covenant, the people of God gathered when the ark, which contained God's glory, entered their presence. "As the ark of the covenant of the LORD came into the camp, all Israel shouted with a great shout [*těruw'ah*], so that the earth resounded" (1 Samuel 4:5). On another occasion, David and the elders of Israel "went to bring up the ark of the covenant of the LORD from the house of Obed-edom with joy [*simchah*]" (1 Chronicles 15:25).

These three—God's presence, the gathering of His people, and joy—all go together. Conversely, when God's presence is withdrawn, as it was numerous times due to Israel's rebellion, happiness disappears. "There is an outcry in the streets concerning the wine; all joy [*simchah*] turns to gloom. The gaiety [*masows*] of the earth is banished" (Isaiah 24:11).

We cannot experience a full portion of happiness if we forsake fellowship with believers. It is crucial that we learn to join in with others to collectively experience God's presence.

Praise

Psalm 22:3 (KJV) says, "But thou art holy, O thou that inhabitest the praises of Israel." People often toss this verse around casually, saying, "God inhabits the praises of His people." This application is a bit sketchy in light of the original language and various translations, but there is ample evidence that the point is valid. Consider the following cross-references:

- "But let the righteous be glad [*'alats*]; let them exult [*samach*] before God; yes, let them rejoice [*suws*] with gladness [*simchah*]. Sing to God, sing praises to His name; lift up a song for Him who rides through the deserts, whose name is the LORD, and exult [*'alaz*] before Him" (Psalm 68:3-4).

- "How blessed [*'esher*] are those who dwell in Your house! They are ever praising You" (Psalm 84:4).

- "Worship the LORD with gladness [*simchah*]; come before him with joyful songs [*rĕnanah*]…Enter his gates with thanksgiving and his courts with praise" (Psalm 100:2,4 NIV).

The phrases *before God*, *in Your house*, and *his courts* are clear indicators of God's presence, and praise is paired with each one. I believe that God's presence and our praise go hand in hand. Of course, you could just try it for yourself. Go to a church service with unfettered praise music and let yourself go. Or try it in the privacy of your home or car. Find a praise song you like and sing along with all of your heart (not just your voice, but your soul). God will be there with you.

A pattern of praise in your life will radically change your attitude and countenance. The active pursuit of His presence is a key component to happiness.

James promises, "Draw near to God and He will draw near to you" (James 4:8). Through the study of His word, prayer, fellowship with believers, and praise, we can draw closer to God and experience His presence. The prophet Isaiah prays, "You shall increase their gladness [*simchah*]; they will be glad [*samach*] in Your presence" (Isaiah 9:3).

Creation

Paul wrote that "since the creation of the world His invisible attributes, His eternal power and divine nature, have been clearly seen" (Romans 1:20). Though we live in a fallen world, we can still see our Creator's power, beauty, and design in nature.

"You make the dawn and the sunset shout for joy [*ranan*]," the psalmist wrote (65:8). When we worship the God who created the universe and not the creation itself, we can discover God's presence in the peaceful setting of a meadow painted with flowers, feel His power in the thundering waves by the ocean shore, and sense His vastness at the top of a great mountain.

When Moses met with God, he ascended a mountain. When Jesus needed to spend time with the Father, he also withdrew to a mountain. Of course, they both sought God's presence, but their example reminds us that by seeking the solace found in His creation, we can all separate ourselves from the distracting influences of the world and experience greater joy.

17

GOODNESS

*Christian, come a little way with me, and I
will teach thee about the way thou must go.*

JOHN BUNYAN, *THE PILGRIM'S PROGRESS*

Like the noun *love*, the adjective *good* as a description of God has
been watered down in the English language. We use it to congratu-
late another team ("good game"), frame a greeting ("good morning"), or
describe something that's merely above average ("good show"). These uses
are accurate, even from a biblical definition, but they fall woefully short
of the glorious origin of a word used to describe the divine nature of God.

- "I will wait on Your name, for it is good" (Psalm 52:9).
- "I will give thanks to Your name, O LORD, for it is good"
  (Psalm 54:6).
- "You are good and do good" (Psalm 119:68).

The proper definition of *good* is "of a favorable character." What more
favorable character exists than our Creator God? Therefore, the ultimate

good is that which is like God. The Hebrew word in these three passages is *towb*, an adjective used hundreds of times throughout the Old Testament. It is translated more than a dozen ways, including *good, right, pleasant, agreeable, glad,* and *happy.* It is used to describe creation, the scriptures, God's works, and of course, God Himself. In fact, in many cases, the word *godly* can be properly inserted in place of *good.* Read it both ways in these passages:

- "You will walk in the way of good [*towb*] men and keep to the paths of the righteous" (Proverbs 2:20).

- "Anxiety in a man's heart weighs it down, but a good [*towb*] word makes it glad [*samach*]" (Proverbs 12:25).

- "Achish replied to David, 'I know that you are pleasing [*towb*] in my sight, like an angel of God'" (1 Samuel 29:9).

- "A good [*towb*] man will obtain favor from the LORD" (Proverbs 12:2).

The word also occurs in the phrase *the tree of the knowledge of good* [*towb*] *and evil.* The word for *evil* is *ra',* which is also the name of the principal pagan god of Egypt. I am not certain, but it may suggest that the knowledge gained through disobedience is not simply learning about right and wrong, but the ability to know the goodness of God equally as well as the evil found in false gods or Satan.

One thing is certain: Goodness, happiness, and godliness are directly correlated, if not synonymous. Three aspects of goodness give us ample reason to be consumed with joy.

God's Goodness Is Unquestionable

We never have to ask God to be good, because it's who He is. "For You, Lord, are good [*towb*], and ready to forgive, and abundant in lovingkindness to all who call upon You" (Psalm 86:5).

When we question God's goodness, we invite worry, doubt, and unhappiness. This doubt is a lens through which life appears confusing and unjust. "If God is good," people ask, "why does He allow bad things to happen?"

This question ignores man's free will and God's inescapable purity. But because God is good, the answer to that question is clear. Suffering occurs as a result of mankind's departure from God and the subsequent sin that came into the world. Exiting Eden brought pain and suffering because it separated man from God. If everyone were good (godly), suffering would cease. That is not to say that every evil action is immediately punished; by the grace of God, we don't always get what we deserve. Likewise, not every good action brings an instant reward. We see things on a microcosmic scale, minute by minute and day by day. But God views the period between the creation of man and the final day of judgment as a work in progress. This is the backdrop of Jesus' statement that the Father "causes His sun to rise on the evil and the good, and sends rain on the righteous and the unrighteous" (Matthew 5:45).

Also, if God tolerated sin in His presence, He would not be good. Evil disinvites God's presence, causing suffering. But in the presence of the Lord, there is only goodness, delight, righteousness, and happiness.

Pairing goodness with the nature of God provides an absolute baseline to define goodness in our own lives. The temptation arises to say that circumstances determine what is good. It is true to say that something may be good for one person but not for another, or good in one case but not in another. It is good for my daughter to wear a dress to school, but not for my son. However, the things that change are the circumstances, not the goodness. God establishes a universal measure for goodness—Himself. Affirming God's goodness is foundational to understanding Him and essential in framing our perception of what brings us happiness.

God's Goodness Is Undeserved

When we draw close to God and experience His goodness, we find something completely unearned on our part. This is grace. From the beginning of time, mankind has experienced touches of God's goodness. Though the Israelites continually broke the old covenant and turned their hearts away from God, He continued to grace them with His presence. This naturally brought them good things. Moses told them, "It is not because of your righteousness that the LORD your God is giving you this good [*towb*] land to possess" (Deuteronomy 9:6).

Paul wrote that "God our Father...has loved us and given us eternal comfort and good [*agathos*] hope by grace" (2 Thessalonians 2:16). The Greek adjective *agathos* is very similar to the Hebrew word *towb* in that it is also translated as "good, pleasant, agreeable, joyful, happy." When Paul quotes Isaiah, talking about the beauty of those who "bring good news of good things" (Romans 10:15), he uses *agathos* where Isaiah used *towb*. In addition to the good news of the gospel, the same adjective is used to describe the law (Romans 7:12), the gifts fathers give their children (Luke 11:13), the works we are created to do (Ephesians 2:10), and God Himself (Luke 18:19). The noun form of the word, *agathōsynē*, is translated *goodness* in the list of the fruit of the Holy Spirit (Galatians 5:22). All of these things are expressions of grace by a good Father.

Paul wrote that we live "under grace" (Romans 6:14) and that this grace comes through Jesus Christ (1 Corinthians 1:4). Again, this is a blessing given to us freely as a result of God's goodness because of who He is, not because of what we have done. When we love God and are called according to His purpose, He makes all things work together for good [*agathos*] (Romans 8:28).

Despite our failure, rebellion, and sinfulness, God continues to extend His grace to every one of us. We are all invited to experience God's goodness, even in our worst state, if we will just reach out to the Father through Jesus Christ. "O taste and see that the LORD is good [*towb*]; how blessed is the man who takes refuge in Him!" (Psalm 34:8).

God's Goodness Is Unending

Buzz Lightyear, the flying astronaut in *Toy Story* and the sequels, was noted for saying, "To infinity and beyond!" The line was humorous because it exposes our inability to comprehend something that never ends. We are finite creatures with a beginning and end through birth and death. That's why it can be difficult to grasp the fact that God's goodness never ceases. We are inclined to believe that just as a parent becomes exasperated with a child, God must grow tired of our neediness. But His goodness goes to infinity—and beyond!

- "Give thanks to the LORD, for He is good [*towb*]; for His lovingkindness is everlasting" (1 Chronicles 16:34; Psalm 118:1; 136:1).

- "Surely goodness [*towb*] and lovingkindness will follow me all the days of my life" (Psalm 23:6).

- "For the LORD is good [*towb*]; His lovingkindness is everlasting and His faithfulness to all generations" (Psalm 100:5).

Believing that God's goodness could possibly end leads to despair. "My eye will not again see good [*towb*]," Job lamented (Job 7:7). He later discovered that he was wrong. The psalmist praised God for His unending goodness. "You have relieved me in my distress," he declares. "Many are saying, 'Who will show us any good [*towb*]?' Lift up the light of Your countenance upon us, O LORD! You have put gladness [*simchah*] in my heart" (Psalm 4:1,6-7).

In our short lifespan, how could we ever believe that we could exhaust the goodness of God? He is who He is forever. We must not fall for the same lie that Job did—that we will not again see goodness. If we are sanctified by the blood of Jesus Christ, we are promised eternal life with God, which means that we are guaranteed to see goodness someday. And if we are to believe Jesus' announcement that "the kingdom of heaven is at hand," we will see goodness in this life as well.

In addition to the documented linguistic overlap of *goodness* and *happiness*, a couple of verses pointedly pair the two.

- "Anxiety in a man's heart weighs it down, but a good [*towb*] word makes it glad [*samach*]" (Proverbs 12:25).

- "He who gives attention to the word will find good [*towb*], and blessed [*'esher*] is he who trusts in the LORD" (Proverbs 16:20).

God's goodness is a sweet, unending gift. Taste of it, and happiness will naturally follow.

The Reality of Evil

Sometimes people don't recognize goodness because they deny the reality of evil. Despite the horrors of Hitler's holocaust, the killing fields of Cambodia, the Soviet Union's gulag, and dozens of other examples throughout history, the seemingly obvious truth that evil exists eludes even some of the most educated people. But when we look at those who are completely empty of any goodness, the evidence does not lie.

Charles Manson is evil because he has none of God's goodness. Osama bin Laden was evil because he denounced the true source of goodness and embraced a philosophy of destruction. Most people live somewhere between the extremes of a Spirit-filled life and the barrenness caused by the complete rejection of God. By recognizing the darkness of evil, we can contrast it with the light of God and see that Jesus Christ is the personification of God's goodness. Then we can experience His goodness by allowing the presence of the Holy Spirit to drive out the evil that encroaches on our souls.

18

HOPE AND OPTIMISM

> *When he has lost all hope,*
> *all object in life, man often*
> *becomes a monster in his misery.*

FYODOR DOSTOYEVSKY, *THE HOUSE OF THE DEAD*

The word *hope* is another victim of popular language. We tend to think of hope as a feeling—often a long shot for something we want. We use it in circumstances that are utterly insignificant ("I hope the birthday cake is chocolate!"), completely out of our control ("I hope it doesn't rain this weekend"), and largely self-centered ("I hope I get this job"). Compare these ideas to the biblical instances of hope, and it's no surprise that we don't really grasp its importance. But it is inextricably tied to happiness, so we must come to understand it. (The conspiracy theorist in me wonders if all of the words listed as the fruit of the Spirit haven't been purposely diluted by nefarious forces, but that is for another book.)

"The hope of the righteous is gladness [*simchah*]," we are told in Proverbs 10:28. Paul tells us to rejoice [*chairō*] in hope (Romans 12:12) and later writes, "Now may the God of hope fill you with all joy [*chara*] and peace in believing, so that you will abound in hope by the power of the Holy Spirit" (Romans 15:13).

So what is hope? Merriam-Webster's definition of the noun form is helpful:

> **1** *archaic*: TRUST, RELIANCE
>
> **2 a:** desire accompanied by expectation of or belief in fulfillment... expectation of fulfillment or success...**b:** someone or something on which hopes are centered...**c:** something hoped for

The trust component of hope is expressed in Psalm 38:15: "For I hope in You, O LORD; You will answer, O Lord my God." This is not a case of wishful thinking. We don't gamble on whether God will respond to us. He will; therefore, we trust Him.

The writer of Hebrews describes the reliance aspect: "This hope we have as an anchor of the soul, a hope both sure and steadfast" (6:19). Paul tells us, "hope does not disappoint" (Romans 5:5). This world is full of disappointment, but true hope is sure, steadfast, and reliable. Paul also refers to the "hope of salvation" (1 Thessalonians 5:8). Again, salvation is not a gamble. It's a promise of God. We can rely on it with our very lives—now and for eternity.

Hope and faith are inextricably linked. "Now faith is the assurance of things hoped for, the conviction of things not seen" (Hebrews 11:1). The expectation appears in references to "the hope laid up for you in heaven" (Colossians 1:5) and "the blessed hope and the appearing of the glory of our great God and Savior" (Titus 2:13). There is a definite assurance here. Heaven is real, and Christ will appear. It's not a matter of if, but when, so you can expect it to happen.

Finally, hope is clearly centered on the Father and His Son. "'The LORD is my portion' says my soul. 'Therefore I have hope in Him'" (Lamentations 3:24). Paul says that Jesus Himself is our hope (1 Timothy 1:1).

This is hope as it relates to God through Jesus Christ. We trust in Him, we rely on Him, and we wait for His promises without doubting. There is no *maybe* when it comes to hope in God. In this, there is certainly happiness. As Paul says, we can "exult [*kauchaomai*] in hope of the glory of God" (Romans 5:2).

But what about having hope in people? Or in the circumstances of this life? We typically use the term *hope* in far less certain contexts, where it can be brutally unreliable. Sure, we can hold on to hope for eternal things, but can we really have a level of hope regarding the difficulties of life?

We can. This is what we call optimism.

Merriam-Webster's offers two definitions of optimism, one that is diametrically opposed to scripture and one that lines up with the Bible. The first definition, "a doctrine that this world is the best possible world," is complete rubbish. This is a hellish concept that, if true, would be the most depressing idea ever conceived. If this is as good as it gets, then either God doesn't exist or He is one twisted cosmic being.

The second definition, "an inclination to put the most favorable construction upon actions and events or to anticipate the best possible outcome," has more relevance to the attitude advocated in the Bible. Still, it has its boundaries. Personally, I like the sentiment reflected in Ecclesiastes 9:4: "For whoever is joined with all the living, there is hope; surely a live dog is better than a dead lion." I may not be as powerful and beautiful as a lion, but as long as this dog is alive, good things can happen!

Optimism is not quite the same as hope, but it is derived from hope. It is an attitude that we choose, despite our circumstances, because we are grounded in an eternal hope that overrides all temporary troubles. To get a good sense of what godly optimism looks like, let's expose three things that it is *not* and then examine three things that it *is*.

Optimism Is Not Fantasy

Optimism expects the best reality without departing from it. We once booked a well-known singer, who was also attractive and single, on the television program *LIFE Today*. Also making an unannounced appearance that night was a man who claimed that God told him to marry her. It didn't take us long to realize that he wasn't simply being optimistic; he was delusional. Granted, God often tells people to do crazy-sounding things, but when God is truly behind something, that is a different matter. When people move to fantasyland on their own, they are not pressing the boundaries of optimism; they have departed from reality.

Optimism Is Not Foolishness

"Know that wisdom is thus for your soul; if you find it, then there will be a future, and your hope will not be cut off" (Proverbs 24:14). We have a responsibility to seek wisdom and understanding. Blindly hoping for things that are not wise or within God's will for our lives is foolishness, not optimism.

Let's suppose you were praying about your job situation and you genuinely felt that God indicated you would become the president of Big-time Corporation. That may sound crazy, but if that's God's plan for your life, He can certainly make it happen. If you walked into the current CEO's office and announced, "God told me that I'm here to run Bigtime Corporation," you would promptly be escorted out of the building by large men in matching uniforms. But if you approached that company and looked for available jobs, you'd be on the right path, both with God and with senior management. You may start in a job below your actual ability and pay scale, but if you were consistently hardworking, wisely optimistic, and honestly pursuing God's will for your life, amazing things would happen. Why? "'For I know the plans I have for you,' declares the Lord, 'plans to prosper you and not to harm you, plans to give you hope and a future'" (Jeremiah 29:11 NIV).

Optimism Is Not Selfishness

Optimism brings personal benefits to be sure, but the motivation cannot be, "What's in it for me?" This is, I believe, where some of the Charismatic community gets off track. I have heard more than a few "name it and claim it" sermons that exhibit a foolish and selfish optimism. The "I'm believing for a BMW" mentality usually signifies selfishness and materialism. You may have a BMW, and that's fine. Nothing is wrong with owning a nice car. But something *is* wrong with pursuing illegitimate desires. We should be optimistic about our needs, God's provision, and His plan for our lives, but not about every selfish desire.

Too many times I have heard the "superman" verse quoted completely out of context. "I can do all things through Christ," people say regarding all manner of selfish things. When Paul wrote that, he was in a Roman prison. Consider the larger context:

> I know how to get along with humble means, and I also know how to live in prosperity; in any and every circumstance I have learned the secret of being filled and going hungry, both of having abundance and suffering need. I can do all things through Him who strengthens me. Nevertheless, you have done well to share with me in my affliction (Philippians 4:12-14).

Paul is telling us to be optimistic, even in the midst of affliction! Whatever your circumstance—out of a job, in the middle of a divorce, on the verge of a breakdown—God can pull you through, not for your glory, but for His. Optimism is designed to make you faithful, not famous.

Now, let's look at three defining characteristics of godly optimism.

Optimism Is Persistent

The pessimist says, "I knew that wouldn't work out the way I wanted." The optimist says, "That didn't work out the way I wanted—let's try another approach." People are flawed, and life is messy. It's easy to be a pessimist. If you're counting on something to fail, you won't be disappointed. If you're looking for the good things in bad situations and hoping for the best, you will have to push through discouragement, failure, betrayal, and other obstacles.

"Let us hold fast the confession of our hope without wavering, for He who promised is faithful; and let us consider how to stimulate one another to love and good deeds" (Hebrews 10:23-24). It's hard to be an optimist without wavering, but when our hope is ultimately in God, we can hold steady. Interestingly, the second half of the exhortation gives us a wonderful motivation to stay optimistic. Our positive attitude will encourage others to love and good deeds. How great is that! Optimism offers dual rewards—it will not only help see us through difficult circumstances but also produce great results in those around us. We just need to stick with it, even in the tough times. "After all," the optimist will say, "things can only get better!"

Optimism Is Patient

Let's face it. When things quickly work out in our favor, it's easy to be optimistic. But the real test comes when the payoff seems as if it will never happen. Paul wrote about this in the context of salvation and redemption. "For in hope we have been saved, but hope that is seen is not hope; for who hopes for what he already sees? But if we hope for what we do not see, with perseverance we wait eagerly for it" (Romans 8:24-25).

Specifically, Paul is referring to his inability to completely overcome his flesh. The problem of lingering sin bothers him, but he's not losing hope because he knows that in the end, all sin will fall away, and God's perfect glory will be revealed in all of those who believe in Him. This is patient optimism. It's not an excuse to avoid dealing with problems, but an assurance that God's plans will eventually prevail in all things. This requires complete trust in God. We have to believe that He knows all things, sees all things, and remains in control of all things. When we fully trust Him and have a long-term faith, we can better maintain short-term faith even when we are tempted to feel as if things will never improve.

Optimism Is Proactive

Happiness is very much mind over matter. It is allowing our attitude to be controlled by our mind, not ruled by our emotions. It does not mean ignoring reality or turning a blind eye to negative things in the world, but believing that "God causes all things to work together for good." There is, of course, a caveat: "to those who love God, to those who are called according to His purpose" (Romans 8:28).

When we pursue God and believe in Jesus Christ, we choose to follow Paul's final exhortations to the church in Philippi:

> Rejoice [*chairō*] in the Lord always; again I will say, rejoice!... Finally, brethren, whatever is true, whatever is honorable, whatever is right, whatever is pure, whatever is lovely, whatever is of good repute, if there is any excellence and if anything worthy of praise, dwell on these things (Philippians 4:4,8).

He tells us to be happy and lists things we can do to achieve that goal. He instructs us to proactively focus on the good things and not be distracted by the bad things. The world is full of bad news and bad people. If we allow our minds to be consumed by these things, we cannot remain optimistic. Zig Ziglar, a great optimist, said, "We all need a daily checkup from the neck up to avoid stinkin' thinkin', which ultimately leads to hardening of the attitudes."

If you find yourself continually pessimistic, ask yourself what the psalmist asked: "Why are you in despair, O my soul? And why have you become disturbed within me? Hope in God, for I shall yet praise Him, the help of my countenance and my God" (Psalm 42:11).

When your hope is in the Lord, you can choose an optimistic attitude, which will have a profound impact on your life and on those around you. Optimism directly affects your happiness, which shows up in your countenance. A genuinely optimistic outlook will enable you to be happier, and that happiness will radiate for all to see.

19

HELPING OTHERS

*If any castaways had landed on the coast, it
was to be feared they were without resources,
and it was therefore the more necessary
to carry help to them without delay.*

JULES VERNE, *THE MYSTERIOUS ISLAND*

Most of us are not castaways. Despite the hardships we face, we have resources—friends, family, neighbors, churches, charities, and other places to seek help. When we shift our focus from our problems to the problems of others, we are reminded of the blessings in our own lives. This is often most visible when dealing with others whose lives are, by comparison, more difficult. This is not to say that we take joy in the misery of others, but that we gain a new perspective when we realize that things could be worse.

An Indian proverb says, "I had no shoes and complained until I met a man who had no feet." I experienced a similar sentiment while facing blindness. Self-pity would have been easy, but during my multiple surgeries, my sister was battling a dangerous form of throat cancer. I wish

139

she never had to face such suffering, both physically and emotionally, but it did make me realize that regardless of how difficult my circumstance might be, it paled in comparison to her life-threatening cancer. Thankfully, my vision was saved and she beat her cancer.

If you are not happy with your life, consider stepping outside of your circumstances to help others who are in pain. Helen Keller said, "Believe, when you are most unhappy, that there is something for you to do in the world. So long as you can sweeten another's pain, life is not in vain."

Working to alleviate the suffering of others not only serves their needs but also takes your focus off yourself. You're not likely to complain about your problems when you're personally involved with someone else's problems. This shift in perspective should restore a level of happiness.

As I combed the scriptures researching the topic of happiness, I came across this passage in the book of Esther: "For the Jews there was light and gladness [*simchah*] and joy [*sasown*] and honor. In each and every province and in each and every city, wherever the king's commandment and his decree arrived, there was gladness [*simchah*] and joy [*sasown*]" (8:16-17).

I wondered what had caused such national "gladness and joy," so I read through the entire book. Esther was an orphaned Jewish girl in exile who, through a series of God-ordained events, became the queen to Ahasuerus, whose reign encompassed 127 provinces from India to Ethiopia. At the advice of her cousin Mordecai, who had raised her, she did not reveal the fact that she was a Jew. During her time as queen, the Jews found themselves once again persecuted, and the king decreed that every Jewish man, woman, and child in the kingdom was to be killed and their possessions stolen.

Given Esther's comfortable position, she could have kept her mouth shut and lived in luxury the rest of her life. She could have taken steps to rescue or hide Mordecai. Or perhaps she could have pursued an Oskar Schindler–style effort to save as many as she could. Instead, she risked everything—her reputation, her position, and even her very life—to save every Jew in the kingdom. She could have been punished as a deceiver for hiding her identity. For all she knew, she would be the first one slaughtered in the coming holocaust. Instead, she found favor and convinced the king to reverse his decree. Her courage saved the lives of an untold number of innocent people, spreading gladness and joy across the land.

There are numerous examples in the Bible and throughout history of people who engaged in acts of kindness to help those in need. They are revered as saints and heroes for good reason: They treated others as their neighbors, just as Jesus commanded all of us to do in His parable of the good Samaritan.

The beauty of this path to happiness lies in its simplicity. All of us can help someone in some way. It just requires stepping outside of ourselves as we give time and effort to improve someone else's life. No measure of service or sacrifice is too small.

It should be noted that helping others involves sympathy (compassion for someone) or empathy (sharing in their pain) but not necessarily a complete assumption of their burden. Psalm 55:22 says, "Cast your burden upon the LORD and He will sustain you." Jesus said, "Come to Me, all who are weary and heavy-laden, and I will give you rest" (Matthew 11:28).

Helping others means meeting some of their needs while pointing them to Jesus. We are clearly told to allow Jesus Christ to take our burdens. Taking others' burdens can hinder our happiness if we are not careful. We shouldn't compound our own suffering with the suffering of others, but join with them in casting all of our cares upon God. He can handle them; we cannot. Presuming that we can meet every need will invite additional and unnecessary hardship. Only through obedience and an overflowing empowerment of the Holy Spirit can we share in and alleviate the suffering of others without being overwhelmed by it.

I remember returning from my first mission trip to southern Africa with a torrent of emotions. I was sickened by the condition of starving children. I was depressed by the vastness of the need. I was also angry at the thoughtless consumption and self-absorption of Americans. I was even disgusted by the behavior of my own young children when they complained about their meals. Working through these negative emotions and finding a healthy balance of grace and compassion took me a while. I have come to the realization that even though God wants everyone's needs to be covered, suffering is an unavoidable part of this life, and we should learn to experience the happiness God wants to impart to us as we live in obedience. When we do this, we find that helping others is as much about entering into the joy of the Lord as it is about impacting other people's lives.

Intercession

When people run out of practical options, they sometimes say, "All we can do is pray." Prayer is treated as a last-ditch effort when our human ability fails. Even Christians fall into this trap because prayer deals with the unseen. It wars against "spiritual forces of wickedness in the heavenly places" (Ephesians 6:12). It focuses on changing people's hearts and minds. But the natural human inclination is to assess effectiveness by immediate, visible, objectively measurable results. So we consciously or unconsciously consider prayer an option only when we're out of all other options.

Praying for others always changes someone, but not always the someone we expect. The relationship between one's free will, predestination, and the power of prayer will remain something of a mystery until we're in the presence of God, but there is no doubt that persistent prayer has a greater impact than the average person realizes. Whether the person for whom we pray responds in the way we wish is out of our control, but that doesn't mean we should not pray.

At the very least, our act of bringing another person's concerns or condition before God changes us. It's hard to hold negative emotions toward people when we're properly interceding for them. In addition, we take our focus off of ourselves. As we carry another's burden to the Lord, He touches us and takes that burden upon Himself. That touch is worth the experience of intercession. It's an open invitation for God to bless us as we share His concern for someone He loves even more than we do.

20

JUSTICE

*Don't you understand the legitimacy of
people's wrath, their wish to live according
to justice, their search for the truth?*

BORIS PASTERNAK, *DOCTOR ZHIVAGO*

On September 11, 2001, Osama bin Laden masterminded the greatest attack on American soil. Almost 3000 people died that day. On the other side of the world, people danced in the streets, celebrating the assault on the "great Satan." Almost ten years later, bin Laden was caught in a Pakistani compound and, after refusing to surrender, shot in the head. That night, Americans danced and shouted in the streets from New York to Los Angeles. To the casual eye, the responses might have looked similar, but they were vastly different for one crucial reason: The 9/11 revelers cheered the loss of innocent lives, but those who rejoiced a decade later applauded justice.

Proverbs 21:15 says, "The exercise of justice is joy [*simchah*] for the righteous, but is terror to the workers of iniquity." Those who celebrated the demise of Osama bin Laden were justified in their happiness, but for evil men who commit murder in the name of their devilish ideology, justice is an enemy.

It is difficult for many people to comprehend the justice of God. Their idea of a loving God does not square with God's intolerance of evil. But throughout the Old Testament, God repeatedly called for a reckoning for those who committed murder, rejected Him, and oppressed innocents. "Righteousness and justice are the foundation of Your throne; lovingkindness and truth go before You" (Psalm 89:14).

God Is Just

A holistic view of the scriptures reveals several truths related to this difficult balance of righteousness, grace, and justice. The first is that God is just. The city of Sodom felt God's wrath because of their wickedness. The psalmist wrote, "Let them shout for joy [*ranan*] and rejoice [*samach*], who favor my vindication; and let them say continually, 'The LORD be magnified, who delights in the prosperity of His servant'" (Psalm 35:27).

Jesus talked repeatedly about an eternal hell, where those who reject Him will reside. Echoing Hosea's observation that evil men "sow the wind and they reap the whirlwind" (Hosea 8:7), Paul said, "God is not mocked; for whatever a man sows, this he will also reap" (Galatians 6:7).

Justice is not an expression of rage or vengeance as much as it is, as Merriam-Webster's defines the word, a "conformity to truth." Sin destroys. Justice allows this truth to take place. If God were to allow all manner of evil to reign without consequence, He would not only be unjust and unfair but also corrupt. Justice requires that the unrepentant sinner reap the consequences of his actions. Yet at the same time, God's desire is that none should perish, but that everyone would enter into His free grace and accept redemption. But He does not force Himself on us.

We Are to Act Justly

God desires justice in our relationships. Several Bible passages describe "differing weights and measures" as an abomination (Deuteronomy 25:13-16; Proverbs 20:10,23). Equality before the law is a biblical concept. In America, we lived the disgrace of inequality throughout decades of slavery and subsequent "Jim Crow" laws. Injustice was reflected very early when "No Irish" signs appeared in New York City as waves of immigrants sought work. The abuse of many Native Americans constitutes a grave abomination. The long and arduous road toward equal treatment has been imperfect and difficult but necessary to attain godly justice. To fully experience the joy that God intends, we must hold up the biblical standard: "How blessed [*'esher*] are those who keep justice, who practice righteousness at all times!" (Psalm 106:3).

We Are to Enact Justice

God commands men to carry out justice on the earth. The Old Testament is replete with supplication and admiration for it. The role of good government includes punishing evil. The book of 2 Kings tells the story of Queen Athaliah, who murdered all of the children in the royal family except for Joash, who was hidden from her. After six years, Joash was presented to the priest Jehoiada. Seeing that an heir to the throne was alive, the priest led the charge to overthrow the evil Athaliah and ordered her execution. The saga ends with this observation: "So all the people of the land rejoiced [*samach*] and the city was quiet. For they had put Athaliah to death with the sword at the king's house" (2 Kings 11:20).

King David wrote this in a psalm commemorating the Israelites' captivity in Babylon:

> O daughter of Babylon, you devastated one,
> How blessed [*'esher*] will be the one who repays you
> With the recompense with which you have repaid us.
> How blessed [*'esher*] will be the one who seizes and
> > dashes your little ones
> Against the rock (Psalm 137:8-9).

This violent expression of justice can be difficult to reconcile with other passages, such as New Testament instructions to never pay back evil for evil (1 Thessalonians 5:15; 1 Peter 3:9). Paul tells us not to take revenge and quotes Deuteronomy 32:35, reminding us that God said, "Vengeance is mine" (Romans 12:19). The chapter in Deuteronomy emphasizes that God will enact justice: "Rejoice [*ranan*], O nations, with His people; for He will avenge the blood of His servants, and will render vengeance on His adversaries, and will atone for His land and His people" (verse 43).

This seems to make clear that civil justice must be part of a righteous society. In practical terms, consequences must be levied for those who steal, rape, murder, and commit other crimes against innocent people. This duty should not be carried out carelessly, but with proper authority and consideration. "Do not rejoice [*samach*] when your enemy falls, and do not let your heart be glad [*giyl*] when he stumbles" (Proverbs 24:17). We should not relish the downfall of those who are punished. Nonetheless, we should exercise justice.

Christians are split over the issue of capital punishment—and for good reason. Certainly those who commit heinous crimes, such as Timothy McVeigh's murderous attack in Oklahoma City, deserve death. But should it come at the hands of other people? I believe that the scriptures give us room to do so. Still, it's a dicey proposition. (Personally, I would be happy if these criminals served a life sentence with hard labor to cover the cost of incarceration.) Regardless of one's opinion on the ultimate penalty, the Bible is clear that a righteous society will reflect God's character and seek justice.

Justice Is a Collective Issue

Individuals are not to carry out their own forms of justice, as in vigilantism. This is where Paul's "overcome evil with good" principle applies. Certainly differing weights and measures would be expressed if each of us carried out our own idea of justice.

On one hand, Martin Luther King Jr. in America and Mahatma Gandhi in India demonstrated the power of nonviolent campaigns for justice. Conversely, Dietrich Bonhoeffer's participation in a plot to assassinate Adolf Hitler illustrates a difficult choice for individuals. Only God holds the authority to exercise justice, but at what point do individuals carry it out while remaining under His authority?

The point could be debated endlessly, but the overarching idea that we treat each other fairly, deal in love individually, and allow certain authorities to prevent and punish evil provides a general framework for happiness. Dealing with particular circumstances requires the wisdom that only God can provide (which is why we see so much injustice, as people reject God's principles and guidance). On an individual basis, we are happiest when we follow the prophet Micah's explanation of what the Lord requires: "to do justice, to love kindness, and to walk humbly with your God" (Micah 6:8).

Leadership

Anyone who has traveled can tell you that cities and countries often emanate their own unique vibes. Before the Berlin Wall came down, I spent a few days in both East and West Berlin. The contrast was tangible. The free West was vibrant and full of life. The Soviet-ruled city was gray and oppressive. The leadership in West Germany was far from perfect, but it was far better than the evil leadership that had dominated the other side of the Berlin Wall since the end of World War II.

Solomon wrote, "When the righteous increase, the people rejoice [*samach*], but when a wicked man rules, people groan" (Proverbs 29:2). Righteous people and leaders contribute directly to the happiness of society. Even when corruption, oppression, and other ungodly values reign, righteous individuals can find joy, as Paul demonstrated from the Roman prison, but it is more difficult. If we truly want to create and disseminate happiness, we will seek to build godly societies and empower principled leaders.

21

PRAISE

*Music has charms to soothe a savage breast, to
soften rocks, or bend a knotted oak.*

WILLIAM CONGREVE, *THE MOURNING BRIDE*

The act of singing to God is supernaturally powerful. The scriptures are loaded with commands to make a joyful noise and sing a new song. The impact of worship with voice and instrument is demonstrated throughout the Bible—from Moses' song of deliverance through the Red Sea, to the numerous songs of praise in the book of Revelation. Of course, praise can be spoken and worship can be exhibited in our actions, but I want to focus on what we currently call praise and worship music.

For me, that translates into the music of David Crowder, Chris Tomlin, Jesus Culture, and other modern worship groups. For others, it translates into hymns, Gregorian chant, or another style. Arguments over musical genres stem from religious and cultural prejudice. God looks on the heart, regardless of what the ear hears. I appreciate the beautiful and poetic lyrics of classic hymns, but whereas that music enthralls some people, it bores me, so engaging with it is difficult for me. Ascribing spiritual significance to a song based on style or age has no biblical basis. Obviously, one cannot worship to music with godless lyrics, but in the realm of edifying, truth-based messages, any style is sufficient. It is even possible to engage in worship by meditating on God's word while listening to instrumental music. Praise is ultimately about the connection it creates between man and God.

"Praise the LORD!" says Psalm 147:1, "for it is good to sing praises to our God; for it is pleasant and praise is becoming." The Hebrew word translated *becoming* is elsewhere translated *beautiful*. And while our vocal ability may not win any awards, it makes us champions in God's eyes. A genuine act of worship does several important things that contribute directly to our happiness.

Worship Makes a Statement

When we genuinely worship in public, we announce to others that we are servants of the Lord. In doing so, we glorify God and humble ourselves. King David exemplified this when the ark of the covenant was brought into Jerusalem and he, the ruler of all God's people, stripped off his royal robe and danced before the Lord "with all his might" (2 Samuel 6:14). Some poor translations imply that he was naked (which would get you arrested and banned from any church nowadays), but he actually wore a linen ephod, which was the garment of the common man. This was not an indecent act, as his wife Michal charged, but an act of humility and pure worship.

King David also brought sacrifices to the altar, blessed all of the people, led them "with shouting and the sound of the trumpet" (verse 15), and handed out treats of cakes and dates. His acts consistently expressed his love for the Lord. The music, dance, sacrifice, generosity, and obedience all declared the kingship of the God of Israel. Coming from the physical king, this was a powerful public statement. When we engage in demonstrative obedience to the Lord, we tell those around us that we acknowledge the kingship of God. This is especially important for men who are husbands and fathers. As leaders of our households, we send a strong message that we are under the lordship of God Almighty. The experience is humbling, powerful, and beautiful.

Of course, our worship cannot be for show. If we think we're going to impress others with our praise, our motives are wrong and our actions vain. It must be pure, genuine, and devoid of self-righteousness. Jesus came at a time when the religious leaders often did things for show. He put this type of thing in its place with the story of the Pharisee who stood in the temple alongside a tax collector and prayed, "God, I thank You that I am not like other people" (Luke 18:11). Whoever treats worship as a show will not receive the blessing that true worship brings. Jesus made the point of the parable clear: "Everyone who exalts himself will be humbled, but he who humbles himself will be exalted" (verse 14).

Worship Redirects Our Focus

Praise and worship also alters our lives in another important way: It shifts our focus from the things of this world to the things of God. One of my favorite worship songs is "All of Creation" by MercyMe. It encourages us to lay down our burdens at Christ's feet as we lift our voices in praise. When we sing to the Lord, we aren't likely to hang on to the worries of the world.

Acts 16 tells of the time when Paul and Silas were beaten and imprisoned for preaching the gospel in Philippi. Most of us would probably bemoan such fortunes. We might question God's wisdom or curse the unbelievers' cruelty. My Baptist friends would wonder whose sin had caused such problems. My Methodist friends would discuss the various saints who had suffered imprisonment through the ages. My Charismatic friends would take authority over the jailers and command the doors to open. But Paul and Silas prayed, and around midnight, they began singing songs of praise.

I doubt the Philippian guards working the graveyard shift were very good-natured. Such late-night serenades may have presented the risk of more bodily harm. And the other inmates, who were certainly not happy with their lodgings, may not have appreciated the disruption. But Paul and Silas were not focused on themselves or those around them. They had shifted their focus entirely to the Lord. The result was earthshaking—literally. An earthquake broke open the prison gates and unfastened the prisoners' chains. At least one jailer and all his household believed in Jesus that night. We don't know the ultimate fate of the other guards and prisoners, but they certainly witnessed the power of God!

Worship Transforms Us

Shifts in our own focus and our acts of praise don't often produce earthquakes, but they do shake the foundation of our souls. When life's troubles warrant grumbling, complaining, or outright cursing, we can refuse to look at our own situation and praise God instead. This changes our perspective and possibly our circumstances. Like Paul and Silas, we may even praise our way out of bondage!

Psalm 89, which begins with the declaration, "I will sing of the loving-kindness of the LORD forever," also says, "How blessed are the people who know the joyful sound [těruw'ah]!" (verse 15). *Joyful sound* is a phrase most often associated with a shout or trumpet blast signaling the presence of God. It's used in both warfare and worship. The second half of the verse says, "O LORD, they walk in the light of Your countenance." Praise alters not only our outlook but also the way we look. When you put a new song in your mouth, you also put a renewed expression on your face.

Those who know that sweet song of worship experience the presence of God in a way that cannot be fully explained. It pierces the core of our being and renews the mind. Praise carries us into His courts (Psalm 100:4) and expresses our joy (James 5:13). It is a powerful weapon against the worries of the world, a reminder of our submission to Him, a witness to the lost, and an invitation for God's presence to inhabit our lives.

22

TRUST

*I an't a Christian like you, Eliza; my
heart's full of bitterness; I can't trust in
God. Why does he let things be so?*

HARRIET BEECHER STOWE, *UNCLE TOM'S CABIN*

The Rocky Mountains are my favorite vacation destination. I live in a
flat, hot, crowded part of Texas, but my heart is at 10,000 feet. Winter or summer, I'd rather be in Colorado. When I drive there from here,
I sometimes take a scenic route that includes a stop at the Royal Gorge.
Spanning the gap more than 1000 feet above the Arkansas River stretches
America's highest suspension bridge. This footbridge is 1260 feet long, 18
feet wide, and will support more than 2 million pounds.

I have boldly walked across this bridge. Why? Because I trust it. I feel
secure and safe, despite the deadly fall that would result from a structural
failure. My wife, who doesn't like heights, hates it. But I enjoy it. Looking
down at the river and around at the mountains brings me a unique joy.
But it wouldn't work without trust. Fear would reign if I didn't have total

faith that the bridge would protect me from certain death. I believe in the integrity of the bridge and trust the engineers who built it and maintain it.

We all exhibit this kind of trust on a routine basis. We drive at high speeds over bridges, ride on elevators that zip us hundreds of feet straight up, work in buildings without fear that the roofs will collapse, and carry on our lives in dozens of other ways that require trust. We even do this despite evidence that such trust is sometimes broken. Structural accidents kill a relatively small number of people each year, but they do occur. Yet most of us rarely even think about such things. We unconsciously go through each day with an amazing level of trust, never questioning the ability or motives of those who design, build, and maintain the structures around us. If only we could trust a perfect God as much as we trust imperfect people!

"O LORD of hosts," the psalmist wrote, "how blessed [*'esher*] is the man who trusts in You!" (Psalm 84:12). The Hebrew noun *'esher* means "happiness, blessedness." Though it's translated here as an adjective, it's actually a noun. The Hebrew verb translated *trust* is *batach*, which is sometimes expressed as being bold, secure, and safe. We may fairly read this passage, "The man who is bold and secure in God will have happiness."

God is more reliable than any man-made structure. When we truly trust God, we feel secure and safe despite the dangers around us. We walk boldly, certain that His foundation is solid. We do not fear. In this, there is happiness. "The LORD is my strength and my shield; my heart trusts in Him, and I am helped; therefore my heart exults [*'alaz*], and with my song I shall thank Him" (Psalm 28:7).

Unlike a bridge we can see, inspect, and test for structural soundness, trust in God requires a different and deeper type of conviction. Complete trust in God is predicated on two important conditions.

God Is Good

While I was a student at Oral Roberts University, I heard the founder declare, "God is a good God!" This simple truth is foundational to the Christian life. If God were not good, He could not be trusted. If al-Qaeda owned Boeing, none of us would ever get on an airplane. If we suspected people held evil intentions toward us, we would not trust our lives to them. To do so would be crazy. That is why many people can't fully trust God—they question His goodness.

"They shall eagerly utter the memory of Your abundant goodness and will shout joyfully [*towb*] of Your righteousness" (Psalm 145:7). God's goodness and our ability to trust Him are inseparable. Worshipping a god who wasn't good all the time would be irrational. We may bow to such a god out of fear, but we would be understandably suspicious of him. Thankfully, goodness is a fundamental characteristic of God. It is His nature, which is why it is part of the fruit of His Holy Spirit's presence in us, and we can trust in Him because of it.

God Is Wise

My kids' school has an annual event in which the students build boats out of cardboard and duct tape. In their science class, they learn the principles of buoyancy and then take a field trip to the city natatorium to test their boats in the swimming pool. They race from one side of the pool to the other, but the real test is whether their boats will stay afloat long enough to make the short trip. Most sink.

These children are far from experts at shipbuilding, and the materials they use are woefully insufficient. Building a boat from cardboard and duct tape is actually possible, but most kids lack the know-how to pull it off. The ones that float barely make it. Despite the students' best intentions, they possess inadequate engineering knowledge and experience.

If God lacked the wisdom to handle all of the storms of mankind, His intentions wouldn't matter. We might want to trust Him, but it would be difficult. Thankfully, that's not the case.

Job affirmed God's wisdom even in his trials: "With Him are strength and sound wisdom" (Job 12:16). Daniel likewise said, "Let the name of God be blessed [*barak*] forever and ever, for wisdom and power belong to Him" (Daniel 2:20). Jeremiah stated that the Lord "established the world by His wisdom" (Jeremiah 51:15). James wrote that God's wisdom is "first pure, then peaceable, gentle, reasonable, full of mercy and good fruits, unwavering, without hypocrisy" (James 3:17).

God is not only wise but also fully understanding of the human condition. We were created in His image, according to His likeness. He is able to search our thoughts and intentions. Through Jesus Christ, who was fully divine and fully human, God experienced the full range of human emotions and physical weaknesses. Jesus was sometimes tempted, hungry, tired, or lonely. He felt pain, sadness, joy, indignation, and betrayal. Though He never sinned, He knows the trials we face. The difference between us and Him is that He conquered them. Now He offers His victory to each of us.

God is both wise and good. Because He knows everything about His creation and desires good things for us, we can trust Him. When we do, we can rejoice through the good times and the bad.

Worry

The subtle enemy of trust is worry. Jesus told us to have nothing to do with it. "Do not worry about tomorrow; for tomorrow will care for itself. Each day has enough trouble of its own" (Matthew 6:34). At another time, He rhetorically asked, "Which of you by worrying can add a single hour to his life's span?" (Luke 12:25).

His point was simple. Worrying does no good. It robs you of your peace and happiness. It doesn't solve problems; it creates them. When we learn to trust God, worry disappears.

23

WISDOM

*The highest wisdom and truth are like the
purest liquid we may wish to imbibe.*

Leo Tolstoy, *War and Peace*

Proverbs 3 is one of the great "wisdom" chapters in the Bible. It is also one of the great passages on happiness. We are familiar with verses 5 and 6: "Trust in the Lord with all your heart and do not lean on your own understanding. In all your ways acknowledge Him, and He will make your paths straight [*yashar*]." The chapter continues, "How blessed [*'esher*] is the man who finds wisdom and the man who gains understanding" (verse 13). It then personifies wisdom: "Her ways are pleasant [*no'am*] ways and all her paths are peace [*shalowm*]. She is a tree of life to those who take hold of her, and happy [*'ashar*] are all who hold her fast" (verses 17-18).

To expand on these ideas, we can look at alternative translations of several of the key words. Find wisdom, and you will possess happiness and blessing (*'esher*), delight, beauty, and pleasantness (*no'am*). Your path will be made straight, smooth, pleasing, and agreeable (*yashar*). You will find peace, prosperity, tranquility, and contentment (*shalowm*). Wisdom will advance you and make you happy (*'ashar*).

So what exactly is wisdom? To get to a good definition, we must first define some terms that are building blocks to achieving it. The first is knowledge, which is the accumulation of information. Next is understanding, or the application of knowledge. Third is discernment—the ability to place value on knowledge and understanding. Finally, we gain wisdom, which is the ability to understand the knowledge we gain and exercise discernment as we apply it.

When my oldest daughter turned 15, we began what's called "parent-taught driver's education." I obtained a curriculum approved by the state of Texas and began teaching her everything she needed to know to be a good driver—at least in theory.

The first step in driver's education is gaining knowledge. My daughter and I read the rules of the road and identified the parts of a car. I explained terms like *merging* and *yielding*. I showed her pictures of signs that indicated when such actions were required. I took her into the garage and pointed out the gas and brake pedals. I told her that the *P* on the gearshift meant "park" and the *D* meant "drive." She soaked it in and soon passed a written test, earning her permit to drive with a parent in the passenger's seat. That's when things got scary.

That's also when she began to gain some understanding. She discovered what it's like to actually push the gas pedal and merge onto the freeway. I'm not sure who was more nervous—her or me. In time, her understanding grew as she put her knowledge into action. Both of us gained confidence in her abilities, yet I knew she was still naive in many ways.

Over time, she began to develop discernment, learning to distinguish between legal actions and smart driving. After another driver's bad decision caused an accident that frightened her terribly, she matured even more. Fortunately, nobody was seriously hurt, but both cars were totally destroyed. As a result, she became a better defensive driver and understood firsthand that even the best drivers can get in a wreck. But for her to truly become a wise driver, she must continually master the knowledge of the rules and vehicle, gain more understanding through experience, and develop an innate sense of safety. This level of driving cannot really be taught. Some drivers never seem to get it even after years behind the wheel.

The same is true in life.

The book of James identifies two types of wisdom: godly and earthly.

The first is supernatural, the second, natural. We can tell the difference between the two because earthly wisdom is selfish, jealous, disorderly, deceitful, and demonic (James 3:14-16). God's wisdom, on the other hand, is "first pure, then peaceable, gentle, reasonable, full of mercy and good fruits, unwavering, without hypocrisy" (verse 17).

If you look at many people who are deemed wise by the world, you will find all manner of ungodliness. Wisdom is used for selfish gain. It's used to cause division and doubt. Some of the greatest "wise men" contradict God's truth and lead people into deception. So if you want the kind of wisdom that leads you to happiness, you must seek godly wisdom. This is what Solomon, considered the wisest man in history, found and extolled.

> Make your ear attentive to wisdom,
> Incline your heart to understanding;
> For if you cry for discernment,
> Lift your voice for understanding;
> If you seek her as silver
> And search for her as for hidden treasures;
> Then you will discern the fear of the LORD
> And discover the knowledge of God.
> For the LORD gives wisdom;
> From His mouth come knowledge and
>   understanding (Proverbs 2:2-6).

This wisdom came to life in Jesus Christ, who spoke and walked in perfect peace, knowledge, and truth. Paul called Him "the power of God and the wisdom of God" (1 Corinthians 1:24). Proverbs 8, like Proverbs 3, personifies wisdom as a woman. It's interesting to note many of the parallels between this personification of wisdom as a person and the incarnation of wisdom in Jesus Christ.

Both called to ordinary men:

- "To you, O men, I call, and my voice is to the sons of men" (Proverbs 8:4).

- "And [Jesus] said to them, 'Follow Me, and I will make you fishers of men'" (Matthew 4:19).

Both speak nothing but truth:

- "For my mouth will utter truth; and wickedness is an abomination to my lips" (Proverbs 8:7).
- "Jesus said to him, 'I am the way, and the truth, and the life'" (John 14:6).

Both love us and make themselves available to us:

- "I love those who love me; and those who diligently seek me will find me" (Proverbs 8:17).
- "He who has My commandments and keeps them is the one who loves Me; and he who loves Me will be loved by My Father, and I will love him and will disclose Myself to him" (John 14:21).

Both existed from the beginning of time:

- "From everlasting I was established, from the beginning, from the earliest times of the earth" (Proverbs 8:23).
- "In the beginning was the Word, and the Word was with God, and the Word was God. He was in the beginning with God" (John 1:1-2).

Both bring blessings to those who follow (note the "happy" words in both passages):

- "Now therefore, O sons, listen to me, for blessed ['esher] are they who keep my ways" (Proverbs 8:32).
- "Blessed [makarios] are those who hear the word of God and observe it" (Luke 11:28).

Both bring the life of God:

- "For he who finds me finds life and obtains favor from the LORD" (Proverbs 8:35).
- "This is eternal life, that they may know You, the only true God, and Jesus Christ whom You have sent" (John 17:3).

To know Jesus Christ is to know wisdom. His words impart wisdom from above, and His actions demonstrate the application of it. Acquiring the knowledge of the Bible, studying it to gain understanding, and allowing the Holy Spirit to impart discernment will develop godly wisdom in us. A personal relationship with Jesus Christ is an intimate experience with wisdom. This is a true and eternal path to happiness.

WWJD?

There was a catchphrase a few years ago that showed up on shirts, bracelets, bumper stickers, and other things: "What would Jesus do?" Though well-intentioned, it missed the real question. Jesus didn't marry, He didn't have children, and He gave His life on a cross. That's not the plan for the vast majority of mankind.

The real question is, what would Jesus have me do? Of course, WWJHMD? doesn't flow so well. We all can emulate the characteristics of Christ and seek to obey His commandments, but we each have different callings, gifts, and roles to play in God's overall plan. As Paul said, "There are varieties of gifts, but the same Spirit. And there are varieties of ministries, and the same Lord. There are varieties of effects, but the same God who works all things in all persons" (1 Corinthians 12:4-6).

He uses the analogy of one body with various parts—hands, feet, ears, eyes—and their diverse functions. This is why wisdom is so critical. Salvation is not a collective experience. We must come to Christ individually and seek His specific will for our lives.

24

A Godly Perspective

*These are conversations with abrupt turns, in
which the perspective changes suddenly.*

Victor Hugo, *Les Misérables*

The Bible tells us to "walk by faith, not by sight" (2 Corinthians 5:7). If you think walking by faith is difficult, try driving that way.

In my midthirties, the retina in my right eye began detaching. If you imagine the retina like wallpaper, it generally begins peeling off the back of the eye from one corner. If it crosses the center of vision, things get troublesome. (If it pulls all the way off, you are blind. There is no reattaching a completely detached retina—at least not yet.) One day I was in the optometrist's office with a small blind spot. The next morning I was at the hospital undergoing serious surgery.

Two small devices, one a light and the other a vacuum-type tool to suck out vitreous fluid, were inserted through the sclera (the white part of the eye), and lasers were shot through my dilated pupil to essentially burn the retina back into place. Recovery required almost two weeks facedown, a tedious and aching process, but the result was nearly perfect.

About four years later, the retina in my other eye started detaching. This time, it peeled back very quickly and crossed the center of vision. This surgery included a *buckle*, which is essentially a band around the eye that squeezes it to relieve pressure from the back of the eyeball. This disrupts the muscles, so for several weeks, my eyes didn't always line up. Aside from the self-consciousness this brings, it causes severe double vision. Rather than opting for another surgery to fix this, I chose to work the muscles back into control. For a while, my vision occasionally split in two, with my left eye seeing things off to the left and tilted at about 20 degrees. This can be disorienting. I kept hitting my head on things and knocking items off tables and counters. I'd see two cups, reach for the wrong one, and knock the real one over.

Driving this way is not recommended, but of course, I drove. I'm stubborn, and I probably made a few angels work overtime. I also gained insight into this idea of walking by faith, not by sight. I figured out that if my vision split, I could not trust what my left eye saw. That's not to say I was blind in my left eye. I could see quite well, but the perspective was off. However, I knew my right eye was true, so I followed that and never got into an accident. Given that faith is "the substance of things hoped for, the evidence of things not seen" (Hebrews 11:1 NKJV), doing things by faith and not by sight took on a new meaning for me.

Faith is not without logic or proof. It has substance and evidence. It is anchored in God's truth. I could see out of my left eye, but if I had followed what I saw instead of what I knew to be true, I would have driven off the road. I learned to drive "by faith" by knowing the difference between truth and impaired vision. When we learn to live by God's truth instead of our impaired human vision, we gain a new perspective—God's perspective.

This is what Paul meant by faith instead of sight. It's not blindly closing our spiritual eyes, but realizing that God's perspective and man's perspective create a sort of double vision. God's word provides substance. Evidence is seen in our experiences when we trust in His word. Operating in the gifts of the Spirit, bearing the fruit of the Spirit, testing the spirits to know what is true, and learning by the testimonies of others all play a part in the evidence of God's work in other people's lives and our own.

- "The LORD has done great things for us; we are glad [*sameach*]" (Psalm 126:3).

- "Do not fear, O land, rejoice and be glad [*samach*], for the LORD has done great things" (Joel 2:21).
- "For You, O LORD, have made me glad [*samach*] by what You have done, I will sing for joy [*ranan*] at the works of Your hands" (Psalm 92:4).

God's work in our lives not only provides evidence of His power and presence but also releases supernatural joy. Learning to see ourselves, others, and the circumstances of life through His eyes changes everything. It puts us on a right course and keeps us from harm.

Through our own eyes, we are weak. Through His, we are strong. When we look at believers, we see sinners. When God looks at them, He sees new creations. The world views the church as homophobic, judgmental, and hypocritical. Jesus sees His bride being prepared for glory. When we look at the world, we see pain, suffering, abuse, and chaos. He sees a field white with harvest waiting to be gathered. When we see bad things happen, He sees an opportunity to work it for good. The list goes on.

Everything is different from God's perspective, and He wants to share it with us. We don't need to wait until we get to heaven to see things as He does. We can learn to walk by supernatural faith, not by natural sight, and to see everything through the pure lens of His perfect will.

Obtaining a godly perspective requires spiritual surgery. We need new eyes. "For now we see in a mirror dimly," Paul wrote (1 Corinthians 13:12). I can tell you firsthand that the worst thing you can do if your retina is detaching is to ignore or deny the situation. If you do, it will just get worse until you're hopelessly blind. Likewise, if people refuse to acknowledge that their spiritual vision is impaired, or they choose to ignore and neglect that fact, it will only get worse. Like Paul, we must first admit that our vision is dim and our perspective askew. Fortunately, there is help.

Every day, I must work to keep my eyes aligned. Ensuring that my vision is correct requires effort. It has gotten much easier the more I have done it, but when I struggle to see, I must refocus. This is true for all of us spiritually. If we're not careful, our natural visual impairment will skew our perspective. We must refocus to see things as God sees them. We must realign our thoughts and attitude with God's word. We must allow the Holy Spirit to correct our outlook. We cannot rely on our own sight. This is the joy of walking (and working, and living, and even driving) by faith. It is the blessing of a godly perspective.

Purpose

Shifting our perspective allows us to find a treasure full of joy—our purpose in life. The eternal question, why am I here? can be answered only when we see ourselves and others through God's eyes. "For I know the plans that I have for you," declares the Lord in Jeremiah 29:11. He has a purpose for every single one of us. Through obedience and faithfulness, we can find and fulfill that purpose. It's never too late to begin, and no purpose is unimportant. Finding meaning in our lives provides a sense of significance and accomplishment.

In a broad sense, the purpose for all of us is to know God and make Him known to others. How this plays out is as unique as each person. That's the amazing thing about our individualism—only you can fulfill God's purpose for you. Nobody else can do it. When that truth becomes reality, the beauty of His unique creation comes to life in a way that is exclusively *you*.

"He has made everything beautiful in its time," the writer of Ecclesiastes said (Ecclesiastes 3:11 NIV). The truest beauty is expressed when you fulfill God's purpose for your life. Even the dirtiest mirror looks bright when reflecting the sun. When you allow your life to become a reflection of His Son, you become the light of the world. When believers lift Him up, He draws all men to Himself. Glorifying God with every part of your being promises a life of purpose and eternal happiness.

25

CELEBRATION

*Fellowship is heaven, and lack
of fellowship is hell: fellowship is life,
and lack of fellowship is death.*

WILLIAM MORRIS, *A DREAM OF JOHN BALL*

In reviewing scripture passages related to happiness and rejoicing, I found an interesting pattern. On numerous occasions, the Lord told people to celebrate and feast. The writer of Ecclesiastes said, "Go then, eat your bread in happiness [*samach*] and drink your wine with a cheerful [*towb*] heart; for God has already approved your works." He called this part of "your reward in life" (Ecclesiastes 9:7,9).

The Old Testament repeatedly illustrates this type of celebration. God evidently likes a good party! In Deuteronomy 16, God instructs His people to routinely observe the feasts of Passover, Weeks, and Booths. These were times to commemorate God's deliverance and provision through sacrifice and celebration. The Israelites were told, "Rejoice [*samach*] in your feast" (verse 14).

In addition to ordained holidays (a word derived from the phrase *holy days*), special occasions were marked in a similar fashion. When David was crowned king over the Israelites, there was great celebration.

> [The Israelites] were there with David three days, eating and drinking, for their kinsmen had prepared for them. Moreover those who were near to them, even as far as Issachar and Zebulun and Naphtali, brought food on donkeys, camels, mules and on oxen, great quantities of flour cakes, fig cakes and bunches of raisins, wine, oil, oxen and sheep. There was joy [*simchah*] indeed in Israel (1 Chronicles 12:39-40).

When Solomon was made king, similar festivities occurred. They involved music and food, and the people made such a ruckus that "the earth shook at their noise" (1 Kings 1:40). At the second coronation of Solomon, the scene was repeated.

> On the next day they made sacrifices to the LORD and offered burnt offerings to the LORD, 1,000 bulls, 1,000 rams and 1,000 lambs, with their drink offerings and sacrifices in abundance for all Israel. So they ate and drank that day before the LORD with great gladness [*simchah*] (1 Chronicles 29:21-22).

Throughout the Old Testament, worship involved celebration—food, drink, music, sacrifice, and fellowship. When Jesus walked the earth, he often "broke bread" with both sinners and His followers. The early church devoted themselves to "the apostles' teaching and to fellowship, to the breaking of bread and to prayer" (Acts 2:42).

When the author of Hebrews urged Christ's followers to purposely assemble together—the "gathering of believers" in church lingo—it is hard to imagine that he was referring to the typical church service of today, where we spend an hour singing a few songs, listening to a sermon, and then shuffling out the doors with perhaps a few shallow words to people whose faces we recognize but whose names we don't know. Of course, not all churches neglect the Old Testament style fellowship. The Southern tradition of "dinner on the ground" and other informal gatherings exemplify the interaction that is laid out in the Bible. It's not just being in the same place at the same time, it is unity of spirit—getting to know each other and forming significant bonds.

I love the old television series *Cheers*. The bar was a place where everybody knew your name, as the opening song claimed. Of course, it was fiction. The characters didn't get drunk and fight or do other things some barflies do. They all looked good while hanging around telling jokes and passing the time. In a way, the shallow relationships between Cliff, Norm, Woody, Diane, Sam and the others was a decent picture of the intention of fellowship. They were "doing life together," as Ed Gungor, my former pastor, likes to say. Every episode was a festival of friendship and good times. That's what biblical celebration should be, except instead of doing it in a Boston basement, we do it under the banner of the Lord.

In modern times, we tend to celebrate Christmas in a manner more consistent with the Old Testament festivals. In America, we also mark Thanksgiving with food, family, and in most Christian homes, prayer. Many also seek to serve others during these times, as is fitting. Some Americans also recognize God's blessings during Independence Day. In countries of British lineage, the tradition of Boxing Day also bears a strong resemblance to the kind of service observed by the Israelites.

The point is that celebration and festivities not only bring happiness but also follow a biblical tradition. It is a perversion of the true intent that such holidays also create stress. This would suggest a misdirected focus. To restore happiness in these times, we need only to look at the things present in the old celebrations and institute them in ours.

First and foremost is worship and sacrifice to the Lord. If there is no remembrance of God's blessings during these times, the spiritual value is lost. Our holidays should be times of gathering with believers not only to feast but also to recall God's work in our lives, teach the stories of the Bible, sing songs of worship, care for the poor, and feed the hungry. In these things, there is joy.

It should be noted that overindulgence in festivity is not scriptural. In today's terms, we call that *partying*. God's people were told to celebrate with food and drink, yet in other passages we are specifically instructed not to be gluttons or drunkards. This would suggest temperance and self-control. In Exodus 23, God gives directions for the festivals of Unleavened Bread, Harvest, and Ingathering. Each occurs once a year. The rest of the year, people worked. Deuteronomy 16 ties work to the celebrations, saying, "God will bless you in all your produce and in all the work of your hands" (verse 15). So while celebration and feasting is a good thing, the festivities have clear boundaries. We must engage in these things under God's direction, with Him at the center. And they must be occasional, not ongoing.

Societies that engaged in godless celebration were rebuked for their debauchery. When the Israelites rejected God, the prophet Amos brought the word of the Lord, saying, "I despise your religious festivals; your assemblies are a stench to me" (Amos 5:21 NIV). The prodigal son squandered all of his father's money on wild living. Clearly there are limits to the celebration.

In short, God-centered holidays should be great sources of joy. Partaking in the blessings of His provision with other believers should be a part of our lives. And sharing this joy with those in need creates an opening for the gospel, shining the light of God's love in a dark world. So work hard—and then celebrate!

FIND YOUR HAPPY PLACE

Second star to the right and straight on 'til morning.

J.M. BARRIE, *PETER PAN*

I hope you'll agree that happiness should be a natural part of the Christian life. If you remove the obstacles to happiness and pursue the paths leading to it, you will reach your destination and find a happy place. Of course, there will always be trials. Your happiness will be tested. But for God's people, there is a light at the end of every tunnel. When you truly possess and express joy, it will help carry you through the darkest times.

"All the days of the afflicted are bad, but a cheerful [*towb*] heart has a continual feast" (Proverbs 15:15). A diligent pursuit of God through a Spirit-filled life will produce a cheerful heart. This, in turn, will be visible in your life. Even when affliction comes, you can still feast on the joy of the Lord.

The psalmist describes God as "the help of my countenance" (Psalm 42:11). The Hebrew word for *countenance* is *paniym*, which literally means "face." The same word appears in Proverbs 15:13: "A joyful [*sameach*] heart makes a cheerful [*yatab*] face." The word *yatab* is not an adjective, as it reads in the English translation, but a verb. In essence, God will make your face happy. (How's that for a daily prayer? "God, make my face happy today!")

If you're not there yet, keep in mind that being happy is a daily decision. The choice is yours. Boldly take hold of the joy God wants for you. Paul wrote, "God has not given us a spirit of timidity, but of power and love and discipline" (2 Timothy 1:7). The word translated here as *discipline* is *sōphronismos*, which is also translated as "sound mind." Your disposition should be controlled by your mind, not your emotions or circumstances. Paul wrote that encouragement from prison in Rome, so he was certainly in a position to be unhappy. But he understood that a positive attitude could overrule a negative outlook.

Your commitment to true happiness will be tested. You will be given the choice daily to pursue joy or slip into discontent. Some challenges will be big. You may lose your job. People may hurt or disappoint you. Money may be tight. Crime may devastate you. Illness may strike. Loved ones will die. But through it all, God promises the grace to bring us through, the peace to calm the storm, and the joy of salvation in Jesus Christ. You must hold on to His promises despite your circumstances.

Not all the tests will be big. Sometimes the small ones trip us up. While writing this book, I have had countless opportunities to forget the words I've written and forsake the truths I've expounded. For example, on the night the Dallas Mavericks won their NBA title, I had been singing and playing at church, so my Saturday was full with rehearsal and the evening service. Afterward, I had dinner with my family and worked late on this book—too late, in fact. I slept a scant three hours before heading back to church early for a run-through and the two Sunday services. I had promised to take my sons to a movie that afternoon, so we went. I managed to stay awake through the movie, but by dinnertime, I was exhausted. I told my wife that my goal was to make it past eight o'clock. After that, the bed was fair game.

About an hour later, my son came into my office and said, "Mom told me to tell you that the neighbors are coming over to watch the game." I must confess, I was not pleased. I like the neighbors, but between my kids, their kids, and the boyfriends who showed up, we had a house full of people for the seven o'clock tip-off. I really don't care about basketball, even when the hometown team is playing for the championship. I hadn't watched an entire game in years.

I had a choice. I could easily justify my displeasure. I wasn't asked if I wanted to host a party. I had already expressed how tired I was. After all, I had been volunteering in church, working on a spiritual book, and fulfilling a promise to my kids. I was due my sleep!

For once, I set my emotions aside. I didn't merely put up with the situation, but consciously chose to embrace it. I decided that if my wife wanted to have a party, I'd enjoy it. And I did. Genuinely. After the game, I told them all goodnight and left them to finish celebrating the Mavericks' victory, but because I chose to be happy, I was. And so was my wife. What could have easily been a point of contention turned into a period of celebration. This is the simple type of happiness we can choose every day.

Once you find your happy place, you will be able to offer happiness to others. Children can give joy to their parents (Proverbs 23:25). Husbands can give happiness to their wives (Deuteronomy 24:5). Paul wrote to the church in Corinth about bringing them sorrow versus making them rejoice. If happiness can be possessed, surely it can be given away.

I was having lunch with a friend one day, and the restaurant service was terrible. The waiter took forever to take our order, refilled our drinks only because we flagged him down, and brought the check without ever asking whether we wanted anything else. He truly seemed as if he didn't care. I was buying lunch that day, and when I paused to calculate the gratuity, my friend asked, "Are you really going to tip him?"

The question was legitimate. The waiter deserved nothing. He didn't earn a dime. But I tipped 20 percent just the same. When my friend laughed and asked why I did that, I replied, "It's not about him. It's about me. I am a good tipper."

That can be our attitude toward happiness. Regardless of what happens, we can say, "It's not about my circumstances; it's about the joy I have in Jesus Christ. I am happy."

The great news about giving happiness is that it reciprocates itself. It has rightly been said that "hurt people hurt people." Conversely, happy people give joy. We can hold on to happiness, share it, and cultivate an environment of joy. Jesus calls you the light of the world. Now is the time to rejoice and let your light shine.

More Great Books from Harvest House

HONESTLY
Johnnie Moore

In his uniquely confessional tone, Johnnie Moore, vice president and campus pastor of Liberty University, leads you on a journey of belief from the hilltop home of the Dalai Lama to a mass grave of more than 250,000 people in Rwanda. He dares to address the doubts and challenges that have turned many well-intentioned Christians into hypocrites. Like a good pastor, he helps heal the wounds he opens, and he leaves you with one question: "What could happen if the world's Christians actually began to live what they say they believe?"

AMAZING ENCOUNTERS WITH GOD
Clayton King

Through these firsthand stories, you will see that you can be amazed by God...as Clayton is after poking around in a dark church basement, meeting a drunken millionaire on an airplane, or having a surprise encounter with the IRS. You'll love this great reminder that God uses ordinary things to reveal Himself.

Dying to Live
Clayton King

This challenge to lay your life down for the gospel examines Jesus' paradox that giving away your life is the only way to find it. Clayton's personal stories reveal why people are drawn to those who are willing to sacrifice themselves for others. You'll be inspired to follow Christ unreservedly.

Breaking Through Depression
Donald P. Hall

Depression can affect you mentally, spiritually, and physically, greatly impacting your life and those you love. With empathy and clear language, psychiatrist Donald Hall integrates spiritual, scientific, and psychological principles in his SMART model that leads you to healing and the good news of God's hope.